GREAT LIVERPUDLIANS

GREAT LIVERPUDLIANS

A fascinating journey through the city's history & the people who made it

David Charters

Great Liverpudlians

Copyright © David Charters, 2010

First edition, 2010

Published by Palatine Books,
an imprint of Carnegie Publishing Ltd
Carnegie House,
Chatsworth Road,
Lancaster, LA1 4SL
www.carnegiepublishing.com

ISBN 978-1-874181-70-5

Designed and typeset by Carnegie Book Production
Printed and bound in the UK by Short Run Press, Exeter

CONTENTS

*This book is dedicated to my wife Alison
and our son Cameron*

Most of the information in this book came from the author's own knowledge, experience and original research, but he would like to thank the staff at the Liverpool Record Office for their expertise and unfailing courtesy. *Mersey Stars (An A to Z of Entertainers)* by Michael Smout was of great help to the author in his preparation of biographies about people in show business. Michael Kelly, the historian and author, was a constant source or help and inspiration. David would also like to thank all his dear friends on the *Liverpool Daily Post* and *Echo*.

PREFACE

Liverpool: City of Immortality

THIS IS NOT A HISTORY IN THE STRICT SENSE, but it is a book packed with information about events and people – our Great Liverpudlians and the part they played in the development of the city.

It begins with a child of the 1950s standing at a bus-stop in Birkenhead on a foggy morning. Those were the days when men would turn to the back pages of their papers to read about football. This enabled me to draw on some heroes from my own memory and tell you about the way I saw them, then and now.

It was always foggy then, but to me fog symbolises the past. It is the theatre of the memory, in which people are held forever. So, through this fog, I journeyed back to the twelfth century and Birkenhead Priory, where the Benedictine monks rowed merchants to the little fishing village of Liverpool, starting the Mersey ferry service.

By the railings overlooking the river, near the Priory, I met Tom Murphy, the sculptor, who has given Liverpool statues of Great Liverpudlians, such as Noel Chavasse, William Ralph (Dixie) Dean, Bill Shankly, Billy Fury, John Lennon, Captain Johnnie Walker, Harold Wilson, Ken Dodd and Bessie Braddock.

Together, we crossed the river, taking the underground train from Birkenhead to Liverpool. On the way we discussed some distinguished men and women and how their lives were woven into the story of Merseyside – the shipyards, the docks, the parks and the resort of New Brighton.

At a café in Liverpool, Tom introduced me to Anthony (Tony) Brown, the painter and guitarist. In 2007, his exhibition called '100 Heads Thinking as One' was the highlight of the celebrations, which marked the 800th anniversary of King John granting Liverpool the Royal Charter (Letters Patent). It enabled the small fishing village to grow into an important port that could be used as an embarkation point for troops bound for Ireland.

Tony's exhibition featured 100 portraits; many of these were of people, who had inspired his own life, friends and members of his family. Inevitably, however, it included famous people as well – Brian Epstein, all four Beatles, actors and playwrights. It has been shown at St George's Hall, Liverpool, Liverpool (Anglican) Cathedral; Liverpool's Metropolitan Cathedral of Christ the King (Catholic); and many other venues, including the lovely Williamson Art Gallery in Birkenhead. Into the background of the portraits, Tony has blended writings and images, telling the viewer about significant places and moments in the life of each individual. Thus, he has provided Liverpool with visual biographies of 100 people.

Accompanying us on this time journey was Ron Formby, then editor of the monthly *Scottie Press*, Britain's oldest community newspaper. It began publication in February 1971. Ron believes with great fervour that Liverpool was built on its communities. Of these none was stronger than the one that developed around Scotland Road in the Vauxhall neighbourhood, hence his paper's name. "A city is its citizens," says Ron and he is right.

I began writing about Merseyside in the 1960s and have always been struck by the loyalty that Liverpudlians have, one for the other. If you make it in this city, you will always be remembered. Perhaps the strongest example of that from recent times is the continuing devotion demonstrated by Liverpudlians to the memory of the 96 men, women and children killed in the Hillsborough Disaster of 1989.

But those who do not respect the affection and admiration of Liverpudlians should beware. Passion cuts both ways.

From these thoughts, I formed the notion that Liverpool was the City of Immortality. This immortality was bestowed on it by the memories of its writers and the paintings and sculptures of its artists. So Tom, Tony and Ron are part of the narrative.

Of course, a book like this is certain to excite controversy. Readers will wonder why some names are in and others are not. Therefore, I should emphasise that his is not a definitive list. It is a personal selection of Great Liverpudlians.

You know, if we're honest about it, Liverpool is quite a small city, but its place in the world is huge. That is why I have written this book.

How to use this book

In the first five chapters, the author takes us on a narrative journey, introducing the reader to important places and people on Merseyside, as he examines the history of Liverpool from mediaeval times to the present day.

Some of these people are indeed Great Liverpudlians. The others have a place in our story. Every person mentioned is listed in the Alphabetical Index with his or her relevant page references.

More detailed information about many of these people is given in the extensive Biographical Index, which lists people in the order of their appearances in the narrative.

Among those introduced are the artists Anthony Brown and Tom Murphy and the community workers Ron Formby and the late Kay Kelly, who played important parts in the development of the book.

Some were, or are, local people. Some played a part in Merseyside's development or influenced the great Liverpudlians. Others simply belong in this book.

David Charters, September 2010

About the author

David Charters was born in 1948 and has lived on Merseyside all his life. Since the mid 1960s, he has been a writer/journalist. His weekly column on the *Liverpool Daily Post* started in 1988 and has run continuously since then, except for a three-year break in the 1990s when he wrote a weekly column for the *Liverpool Echo*. David is also a regular guest on the Linda McDermott show on Radio Merseyside. During 45 years in journalism, he has won numerous awards.

© ANTHONY AND LORRAINE BROWN
EMSO ARTS

His publications include *Liverpool: The World in One City* (2003, a thematic compilation of his articles about Liverpool's history, which had first appeared in the *Daily Post*) and *Life, Love and Washing Up* (2006, a compilation of his humorous columns).

These days, David is much in demand as a public speaker.

LIVERPUDLIAN: A DEFINITION

Dictionaries define "Liverpudlian" as a native of Liverpool. The use of "pudlian" instead of "poolian" is generally thought to have been a jocular combination of liver and puddle dating from the 1830s.

1

IN THE BEGINNING

M IST HUNG OVER THE RIVER THAT MORNING – not like it did in the old days of tender memory, when the orange street lamps seemed to float on the veiled air, dangling from a sullen sky, one after the other in measured parade, glowing bodiless and ever more feebly into the distance.

It was natural then to think you were alone in the fog, hands in pockets, collar high, yawning, sweet tea on your thick breath – until a match rasped on the wall a few feet away.

There was a man in a hat cupping his hands to save the flame, which he raised to the cigarette in his lips, before coughing. Dark phlegm groaned in his chest.

Everyone smoked and everyone had a cough in those times. It was the dawn chorus in a town, where car lights crept forward, gingerly, and windscreen wipers flapped in a vain effort to polish visibility into the murk. Bicycle bells sounded, engines wheezed, children chattered, young women tightened their headscarves and rubbed their chilblains on lofty-heeled shoes and everyone at the stop outside the old bank knew the blue bus would be late. What else could you expect in a fog like that? All you could see was your breath.

I stood there holding the back page of the daily paper close to my eyes, so that I could read a report about my hero Dave Hickson, the centre forward at Everton, wearer of the number nine shirt. The football reporters, who covered the big matches at Goodison Park, home of Everton, used such wonderful words to describe him – Dashing Dave, Daring Dave, the Cannonball Kid and the Blond Bombshell.

"Gosh," I thought, "I'd like to write for newspapers making these stories live for millions of readers."

Everyone, who followed the blue of Everton, rather than the red of Liverpool, loved Dave. "Davy, Davy Hickson, King of the Football League," we sang to a tune, which had been much in favour a few years earlier in 1955, when Walt Disney's studio had made a film, starring Fess Parker, about an American, brimmed with cracker barrel wisdom, courage and backwoods' philosophy, all contained under his racoon skin cap. He was called Davy Crockett – "Davy, Davy Crockett, King of the Wild Frontier".

And then in further celebration we mimicked the second line, "Born on a mountain top in Tennessee", with, "Born on a mountain top in Ellesmere Port".

It was a small town on the end of the Manchester Ship Canal, about 12 miles from Liverpool, but it grew rapidly in the 1960s on the back of the oil industry and the Vauxhall car factory built on an old airport. Dave had attended John Street School there. All the other lads could tell he was going to be a fine footballer and he was soon playing for Cheshire Boys. A love of the game pumped in his heart.

He was a modest chap with a surprisingly gentle local accent, but if he had looked longer in the mirror, he would have realised that God had fashioned him as a hero – blue-eyed, broad-shouldered and tall with a mane of blond hair swept back from his forehead. In 1948, he was talent-spotted by the Everton manager Cliff Britton, who signed him.

Dave's early career was interrupted by two years National Service with the Army, where he had been in a cadets' team coached by Dixie Dean. Well, everyone called him "Dixie" Dean, but his real name was William Ralph Dean. He had been brought up in Laird Street, Birkenhead, near the docks, about a mile away from the foggy spot where I was standing, waiting for the bus.

Dixie was what the reporters called a "legend", the greatest English centre forward in the history of the game. In the season 1927/28, he had scored 60 League goals for Everton, a record, which will never be broken.

Old-timers spoke of how Dean had needed to score three against Arsenal in the final match of the season to secure the total. He had scored two, one a penalty, and then with only five minutes to go Everton were awarded a corner. The wily winger Alex Troupe, all five feet five inches of him, took it. He could have picked out Dixie's head if he had been blindfolded in a fog as thick as this one, but he was in the comparatively clear air at the Stanley Park end of dear old Goodison. The ball seared through that air, followed by more than 120,000 eyes. Dixie leapt. The muscles on his neck swelled, as his great head directed the ball into the back of the neck, sweet as you like.

The noise was thunderous. Some wag said you could hear them in the city centre – Chester, that is. Well, everyone likes a good story, but you could certainly hear the celebrations in Dean's native Birkenhead. Ah, dreams. We love dreams on Merseyside.

But another story was even more exciting to me. In February 1953, Everton, then a Second Division team, were drawn against Manchester United in the fifth round of the FA Cup. Almost 78,000 people crammed into Goodison Park. United took the lead, but Tommy Eglington equalised. The ground heaved. Steam and smoke formed a cloud over the famous Gwladys Street end, the terraced temple of Evertonians. Dave dived for a ball to head his side into the lead. Instead, the boot of a defender gashed his sweating brow. Blood gushed from the wound, which was stitched in the dressing room by Harry Cooke, the veteran trainer/physio with the "magic" fingers.

Even this huge, wildly partisan crowd was astonished to see Dave return to the field. This was Hannibal crossing the Alps. The romance was sealed when he shot home the winner, but then, in the dying minutes, he rose from a melee to head the heavy leather ball. The wound reopened and blood splattered on his blue shirt.

Roy of the Rovers, who would make his debut for Melchester Rovers on the front page of the *Tiger* comic in 1954, had been anticipated in flesh and blood by Dave of Everton.

"Hey, son it's here," said an old chap, bumping my shoulder.

"Eh, what?" I said replied, still in a reverie.

"Wake up! The bus, the bus is here! You were miles away. Go on, step on it."

Yes, the fog and smog seemed permanent then, coating lungs with a gripping poison. You could hear the tight breath of hollow-cheeked men and women, in their early sixties with coffin-brown skin and nicotine-stained fingers. But there was romance in the fog as well. Ghosts could live there and you would never see them at all. Fog was the theatre of stories.

Life changes, though. The air is clean now and you can see the day in front of you and all that God and man have to offer us. Sooty layers have been scrubbed from the great, shimmering buildings along the waterfront on the opposite side of the river; or simply "the other side", as local people always say in a tone, which suggests a divide that is not merely geographical.

Anyway, you could see these buildings, through the rising mist of this new morning, when, as a 62-year-old man, I stepped to the banks of the river, near Birkenhead Priory, the oldest building still standing on Merseyside. Hadn't the jokers always said that the best thing about Birkenhead was the view of Liverpool? Scouse wit, cynical, mocking and often true.

Three quarters of a mile away, right across the swelling water, they stood – the Royal Liver Building (1911), home of the Royal Liver Friendly Society – topped, of course, with the two mythical birds, ancient symbols of the city; the Cunard Building (1916), former headquarters of the great Cunard Shipping Line; and the Port of Liverpool Building (1907), formerly home of the Mersey Docks and Harbour Board.

This is the Liverpool that people know, the postcard port, reaching back to the days when it was the second city of the British Empire. "Which was the first?" asked the kids, all wide-eyed and innocent. It certainly wasn't Manchester, our grim-visaged rival for domination of England's north west. That was for sure.

They call those buildings the Three Graces now, but I don't remember that name being used in 1958, when I was 10, reading the *Liverpool Daily Post* football pages on the bus. It seems contrived – something that would slip off the tongues of advertisers or publicists, rather than the true local people.

Alongside the grand buildings are the modern skyscrapers, hotels and apartments, which supposedly symbolise the renaissance of Liverpool, loudly and enthusiastically expressed during 2008, its year as the European Capital of Culture.

But as the young sun pierced the fading mist and spread patterns on the water, I found my mind wandering back, down the centuries. Sounds and pictures came to me that I had never heard or seen before.

All the boys and girls of Merseyside are taught about the Priory and how the Benedictine monks there rowed merchants across the river to the fishing village of Liverpool, thus starting the ferries across the Mersey. The Priory was founded around 1150 by the Norman landowner, Hamon de Masci (his name has various spellings), third Baron of Dunham Massey (or Masci). It was visited at least twice by Edward I, who was impressed by its location, which could be used to further his ambitions in Ireland and Wales.

In 1317, he issued a licence, giving the hooded oarsmen the right to accommodate those waiting for a boat. Crossings were quite perilous and

A view across the Mersey from Wirral
© AUTHOR

would not be risked in poor weather. The
licence was granted in recognition of a
petition submitted by the prior, Robert
de Waley. It said:

> "To our Lord the King and to his
> council pray his poor chaplains the
> prior and the convent of Birkenhead
> in the County of Chester, which house
> is situated on an arm of the sea where
> there is a common ferry (passage)
> between the Counties of Lancaster
> and Chester, that there is no lodging
> place for those passing over the water
> day by day. May it please our Lord the
> King that they may build some houses
> as lodgings at the ferry and sell food
> to passengers there."

The monks built hostels on a site in what is now Water Street. A settlement
grew around the Priory and it became renowned for its hospitality. Those
were lusty times and many appetites were satisfied there, just a few yards up
the road from the place where I was watching the river.

The licence was repeated by Edward II and on April 13, 1330, Edward III
granted a charter to the monks giving them and their successors:

> "The right of ferry over the Arm of the Sea, for men, horses and other
> things whatsoever and may receive for that Passage what is reasonable
> without let or hindrance".

Some school children might have read the charter in the original Latin:

> "Quod ipsi et eorum successores impertuum habeant ibidem dictum
> passagium dictum ultra brachium maris tam pro homnibus quam pro
> equis et allis rebus quibuscunque et pro passagio ill recipiant raciona-
> biliter prout fuerit faciendum sine occasione vel impedimento."

The monks would have been rowing across the Mersey from the early days
of the Priory, but that gave them the royal stamp of approval.

I stood at this place thinking of how holiness and prayer can be reduced
to a lesson in a classroom or a few paragraphs in a travel brochure. The wind
blew a little harder and a chill puckered the water, beneath the railings. My
mind wandered into a picture …

St Mary's tower pierces the sky by Birkenhead Priory
© AUTHOR

Monks with the taste of fish in their mouths are sitting on rough benches in the Chapter House, silently reading from the Bible, overlooked by the Prior, who hovers by the arched window. One, an old chap, whiskered and stooped, rubs his thumb against a knot on the wood. This thumb had rubbed some foreheads in its time, easing people on their way to God. Only yesterday there had been that little girl, the cobbler's daughter. She had never been strong enough for this world and then the coughing sickness came. Outside the river rinses the reedy shore, birds hunch on the trees behind the scriptorium, where the friars write holy tracts; gulls bicker, tunics are swishing among the reeds; gargling melodies are played in the little streams rushing over the stones to the big river; booted feet gloop deeply by the sighs of drying mud. Young sheep bleat and a new baby yells, as an old woman is bound in coarse sacking, so that she can be carried to the burial ground; life goes on – distant hammerings, plainsong, curses, the moan of cattle and knees bruised in prayer. But the ladies of pleasure still sleep.

I closed my eyes to save the picture.

The ferries, which had been given their charter by a king, advanced from oars and sails to steam and onto diesel engines. They still run today, joining Liverpool's Pier Head with the landing stages at Birkenhead Woodside and Seacombe.

The most celebrated crossing had been between Liverpool and New Brighton. It's part of our folk history. In 1948 alone, the ferry carried more than eight million passengers to New Brighton, a trip of two and three-quarter miles. Don't be mistaken here. Many of them were the same people making the journey time and time again, but it remains an impressive figure. New Brighton was redeveloped with a modernised Floral Pavilion theatre, shops and dwellings in 2208/9, but it remains a haunt for our memories.

In 1830, James Atherton, a builder from the Everton district of Liverpool, had the dream of developing a holiday resort on the Mersey that would have all the grandeur of old Brighton in Sussex.

Atherton was the eighth of 10 children born at Ditton, near Widnes, to the farmer William Atherton and his wife Margaret. As a young man he set himself up in business as a grocer and in 1792 he married Betty Rowson at Grappenhall Parish Church, near Warrington. They moved to Pool Lane. Liverpool, later settling in South Castle Street and then James Street, before building their own house near the old Everton Beacon in what was a rapidly growing port. Atherton had established himself there as

Birkenhead Priory, first home of the Mersey ferries
© AUTHOR

a builder and merchant. In the second half of the eighteenth century, the slave and textile trades had led to a huge growth in Liverpool's population and prosperity. In 1716, Liverpool handled a 24th share of England's cargo tonnage. By 1792, it was handling a sixth of the country's tonnage.

These were heady days for the town, deeply stained by its part in the slave trade, an infamous and shameful period of history. It has been widely discussed and rightly condemned in other publications. Really, there is little to add.

Atherton would seem to have been filled with the spirit of the age – a man of business, religion and robust desires. He and Betty eventually had nine children. So the family needed even more space, which they found in a grand house in Northumberland Terrace.

When the Parliamentary Bill for the Abolition of Slavery received Royal Assent in March 1807, Atherton was involved in various property enterprises, as well as building projects on land that he had acquired on the St Domingo Estate, Everton.

After building a house for his family, on the high ground near the old Everton Beacon, he laid out a new street close by and named it Albion Crescent. In common with many rich merchants, he had realised that life in the sweating, throbbing city was unhealthy. The new middle and professional classes would wish to move into the breezier suburbs, in which he concentrated many of his buildings. Between 1812 and 1814, he was the prime mover in the building of St George's Church, near his home on Northumberland Terrace. It was popularly known as the Iron Church because of its stone exterior and cast-iron interior. John Cragg was the builder and Thomas Rickman the architect.

It is worth pausing the narrative here to remind people of how Liverpool had been transformed from its modest origins as a small fishing village. In 1750 the population was only 22,000, but by 1801 it was 77,500, peaking at about 855,000 in the 1930s. It is now (2010) around 450,000.

But back to Atherton, who loved the site of his church in Everton with its grand view over the Mersey to the clean shores of Wirral. By 1823, he was a very wealthy chap, able to retire from day-to-day activities in Liverpool. However, a seething ambition to leave his mark on Earth had not diminished and seven years later he began the project for which he is remembered in history.

Atherton bought 170 acres of sandhills and heathland, where he planned a resort, which would afford residents an unbroken vista across the river. His project was centred on building the Royal Lighthouse Hotel and a steamboat to ferry passengers to and from Liverpool. His idea was to raise the £12,000 needed in shares of £100 each. To this end, he prepared a prospectus for potential investors. Although the Mersey is no longer polluted by sewage and industrial and chemical waste, as can be seen by the many anglers dotted along the front on both banks, you may still be surprised by the glowing tone of his words.

"As a bathing place, it has a particular advantage, not only of being the nearest point to the open sea, but it also possesses a most beautiful beach, the sands are hard and clean – the tide never recedes more than 200 yards from the land. New Brighton also possesses a more interesting sea view than any other watering place can boast, being constantly enlivened by the passing of vessels to and from Liverpool. It is intended to erect a church, market place, baths, billiard room, post office etc. Indeed, nothing will be left undone to make it a most attractive and fashionable watering place. Under such circumstances the hotel and ferry must combine great advantage. Strangers will prefer shopping here, as they can at once get into a packet without inconvenience."

Atherton's New Brighton soon bloomed in gaudy colours and I thought of what was to me the old New Brighton, as I leaned on the railings at Birkenhead Priory.

I could almost touch it, see it and smell it. Yes, New Brighton exists in the present and looks for a future, but it also lies among the pictures of the mind. I see memories and ghosts linking arms to stroll down the prom, again. To be in a resort out of season, when the carousels are frozen, the dodgem cars shackled and the laughing clown is dumb and still, is to glimpse another England, forever gone. But it may make you smile and shake your head at the way we were then, whatever your age now.

Ssshh. It's still there – the smell of vinegar on the chips. Can you see the little girl with candyfloss-encrusted hair? Whipped sand stings your eyes and you can hear the swell of the Wurlitzer organ, the harsh call of gulls and the slap of sandals on the old pier.

"Give us a kiss, love. Just one, go on."

Teddy boys skulk in the doorways with greased hair and padded shoulders, eyeing the girls with lacquered beehive hair and suspenders under their dresses, or "suzzies", as they were affectionately known to generations of garter-snappers. Babies were made in New Brighton, where vivid letters still seep through the sticks of rock.

By the end of the nineteenth century, it was a serious rival to Blackpool, whose main attraction was a tower of 518ft high, which had opened to the public in 1894. Two years later, New Brighton Tower was under construction. It opened to the public in 1900. It was 567ft and billed as Britain's answer to the Eiffel Tower in Paris (984ft). But the New Brighton Tower and Recreation Company had a problem in common with all British resorts. The number of visitors fell off drastically in the winter and that could not be fully offset by indoor attractions.

"What about football?" asked the businessmen. Everton and Liverpool over the water both attracted big crowds and the game, first played in English public schools, was popular with working-class men right across Lancashire. A huge stadium had already been built alongside the tower.

In 1897/98 New Brighton Tower Football Club joined the Lancashire League, gaining promotion to the Second Division of the Football League the following season. There was plenty of money about; in a bid to prosper further, the club signed new players, including some who had played international football. The policy seemed to work and Tower FC finished fifth in its first season, and fourth in the third season. Support was the problem. Big matches attracted crowds of up to 10,000, but attendances for the less glamorous fixtures fell to fewer than 1,000.

The Tower's owners disbanded the club in the summer of 1901. It was replaced in the Football League by Doncaster Rovers. In 1921, New Brighton FC, which had no connection with the old club, was formed. It played in the Football League from 1923 until 1951. The tower itself was demolished in 1919, ostensibly because it had become unsafe as a result of neglect during the Great War, though few locals believed this, as it seemed to be a remarkably sturdy structure. The metal was sold to scrap dealers. In 1969, the glorious Tower Ballroom, which had been part of the same complex, was destroyed by fire.

New Brighton was plagued by problems throughout the twentieth century. In 1868, a pleasure pier had been built. At 550ft and 70ft wide, it was not as handsome as those jutting from other resorts, but it provided a place of entertainment and gentle exercise. It was rebuilt in 1931 and then stood until 1978 when it was demolished after a public inquiry, which had judged that it was not of any particular architectural merit. Seven years earlier, the ferry service from Liverpool had stopped because of silting in the river.

A little further up the coast from the site of the old tower is Fort Perch Rock, one of the most extraordinary structures on Merseyside. It had been built in the late 1820s in the wake of the Napoleonic wars as part of our coastal defences. The construction was carried out under the direction of captain John Sykes Kitson of the Royal Engineers. It had 18 guns, 16 of them 32-pounders. The fort occupies 4,000 square yards. The original walls were 24 and 29 feet high, some were increased to 32ft with the towers reaching 40ft. The fort went into action twice – on the outbreak of the Great War (1914) when a round was fired across the bow of a Norwegian sailing ship, which apparently ignored a signal from the fort, then occupied by Territorials under the command Major Charles Luga, a dentist. Fortunately, the elevation of the gun had been far too high and the shell whizzed across the river, landing in the sandhills at Crosby. A resident strolling along the beach found it and calmly took it to the nearby Seaforth Battery, where it was later tagged, "A Present from New Brighton".

On the outbreak of the Second World War in 1939, there was a similar

incident. A fishing-smack came up the Rock Channel. Colonel Charles Cocks, the battery commander, ordered two shots to be fired across her bows. The owner of the fishing-smack was ordered to pay £25 for each round.

Soon, though, a more dreadful price would be paid by our shipping. Liverpool became the headquarters of Western Approaches, commanding the Battle of the Atlantic, the only campaign to last the six-years of war. German U-boats were trying to prevent supplies reaching our shores from the USA and parts of the British Empire. The Allies lost 30,248 sailors, 3,500 merchant ships and 175 warships. Some 28,000 German sailors died and 783 submarines were destroyed.

The military uses of Fort Perch Rock ended in 1951. Its condition deteriorated until the late Norman Kingham bought and restored it, introducing the items collected into a war museum. In 1997, he sold it to Doug and Alice Darroch, both of whom died in 2006. It then passed to their children Dougie, David, Alison, John and Duncan. Fort Perch Rock now houses museums to Elvis Presley and Merseybeat, as well as the wartime memorabilia and relics, including part of a Spitfire, which crashed in Birkenhead Park in 1942.

It is also a venue for rock, jazz and blues concerts.

I love New Brighton, still seeing it as I did as a child. Something has been lost there and it will never be found again. If you need a word to symbolise this feeling, it's soul – the grey, intangible images on old photographs, the pictures of smiling dads and mums, the parades of kiss-me-quick-hats and the old men at the magnificent open-air swimming pool, reaching for their cameras, as the beauty queens in their hugging costumes twirled and the panel of Miss New Brighton judges in their candy-striped blazers smiled over their gleaming dentures and winked their "I'll-see-you-later-eyes".

A cream tea was served to the winner and her parents and it was a very 'refained' affair with delicate cups and crooked little fingers. The charm was profound. If New Brighton had remained as successful as Blackpool, Torquay, Morecambe or even Southport, I wouldn't have felt so deeply about it. The more it faded, the more vivid it became to me.

"You're thinking very deeply," said a stranger, who had joined me at the railings looking over the Mersey from Birkenhead. He paused to roll his own cigarette. "Still allowed to smoke here," he continued, referring to the legislation, which had banned all smoking in public buildings. I smiled. There was something of the rebel in that voice which appealed to me. There was also something very familiar about it. I looked again. The mist was lifting.

"Oh, I'm sorry," I said. "I was thinking so deeply that I didn't recognise you. My mind was miles away. Well, in New Brighton to be more precise."

"All that thinking will ruin your health," he said. "Anyway, your wife said I'd find you here. She said you were doing some research for a book. More likely you're just on the skive from household duties."

"Hhmm," I said smiling again. "You know me."

But you don't know yet that this man beside me on the railings was Tom Murphy, the sculptor. I had once described him in a newspaper article as, "The man who gave Liverpool its immortality".

I was struck then by the fancy that people who had been written about, sculpted or painted never really died. Of course their real lives had gone, but the artists had given them back to the people, so they had a kind of immortality.

If this was true Tom had certainly done his bit. Among the great Liverpudlians he has sculpted are Harold Wilson, Prime Minister; Dixie Dean; Bill Shankly, the football manager who revived Liverpool FC; Noel Chavasse, doctor and hero of the Great War; Johnnie Walker, hero of the Battle of the Atlantic; John Lennon and the other Beatles; John and Cecil Moores, brothers behind the Littlewoods pools empire; Billy Fury, Liverpool's first great rock and roller; Ken Dodd, the finest stand-up comedian of his generation; and Bessie Braddock, political stalwart of the people, whose wobbling jowls alarmed prime ministers. He also gave us the war monument on the Pier Head.

"Do you fancy a nice cuppa, in a café I know?" Asked Tom. "There's a chap I'd like you to meet."

2

THE BRUISED MESSIAHS

So we crossed the Mersey from Birkenhead to Liverpool that morning, not on the ferry like the monks of faded days – but on the train, following the vivid commuters of this age with their briefcases and light scents.

About a quarter mile up the hill from the priory is an underground railway station called Hamilton Square. Immediately above it is the square of Georgian terraces from which it took its name.

This splendid development of houses, suited to the professional and merchant classes, was begun in 1826 to a design by James Gillespie Graham, an eminent Edinburgh architect. In the middle was a network of lawns and flower beds, criss-crossed by paths, along which haughty-nosed nannies in starched uniforms and shining faces once pushed high-sprung, hooded prams, containing the sons and daughters of the house-owners, whose tall, grey homes looked over the river to Liverpool. It was then a fine and uncluttered view of the Mersey in its full pomp, enhanced by gracious liners and dutiful cargo ships.

William Laird, a Scot, who started the Birkenhead Iron Works, had bought the land two years earlier, naming it after his wife's family. Laird envisaged long, wide and straight avenues lined by these elegant houses in a style, which would have been familiar to him from his time in the Scottish capital.

But the handsomely whiskered Laird is even more renowned for his iron works that soon expanded to meet orders for ships to serve the expanding British Empire. Liverpool was not yet complete master of the Mersey and thrusting Birkenhead, calling itself the City of the Future, was a serious rival with its growing industry and deep docks.

The town's ambition would be demonstrated to international acclaim in 1847 when the magnificent 226-acre Birkenhead Park was opened. The great

Joseph Paxton, who would later design the Crystal Palace in London, laid it out with lakes and serpentine paths. It was the first park in the world to be built by public subscription, with the sale of the impressive houses around it helping to meet the costs, while also engendering a spirit of civic pride.

Under the guidance of his son, John Laird, who had joined in 1828, the yard grew in reputation and output. In 1903, it merged with the Sheffield steel manufacturing company of Charles Cammell to become Cammell Laird Shipbuilders. Fine vessels to sail from Birkenhead include the *Rodney* (1925) and the *Prince of Wales* (1941), both of which took part in the mission to sink the *Bismarck* in the Second World War; the Ark Royal aircraft carriers (1938 and 1950), and the liners, *Mauretania* (1938) and the *Windsor Castle* (1960); as well as the nuclear submarines, *Renown* and *Revenge*, in the 1960s. When the order books were full, the yard employed nearly 20,000 people. Before leaving Birkenhead, I gazed back at the green-domed town hall, overlooking the memorial to those killed in war.

Work on the town hall, made from Scottish granite and local sandstone, started in 1883, opening four years later. It was designed by the architect Charles Ellison. The dome has made it one of the most distinctive buildings on this side of the water. In its prime, it had been a place of grandeur with a marble stairway, stained glass windows depicting great figures from history, and magnificent stone floors in the classical style.

Here, men of prominence made the big decisions about the town. Clerks

Birkenhead's old
town hall crowns
Hamilton Square
© AUTHOR

with winged collars heeded their words, which would later be typed by pert secretaries and slipped into the files of doom, never to be read again. Mayors in chains and red gowns strode the corridors, stalked by the cunning aldermen, who saw opportunities for expansion, where other people saw beautiful fields.

As a cub reporter on the *Birkenhead News*, which appeared twice weekly in those days and was bought by almost every household, I had visited the town hall many times, notebook at the ready, shoes polished, but eyes wary. Grand balls were held for the best people in town and paroxysms of jealousy passed through the committees of the golf, tennis and Rotary club, and the professional societies, when the invitations were announced and certain names were not included.

The catering, a little unexpectedly, was entrusted to the Birkenhead and District Co-operative Society in deference to their excellent spreads of salmon slices, Spam and sherry trifle, as well as the town's strong socialist ethos of grazed knees and hard fists. In 1974, Birkenhead was absorbed into the new Wirral Borough Council and the seat of power was switched to Wallasey Town Hall, a couple of miles up the coast. After years of indecision, the old town hall was turned into a museum and its future is now uncertain.

"Sometimes I wonder if we're all in a museum now," I said to Tom, but he just smiled as we strode towards the railway station. By then the mist had vanished completely. Across the road from the station, there used to be a café called Olivieri's run by an Italian family, who had come over from Viareggio earlier in the twentieth century. It sold milky coffee and frothy coffee, as well as many styles of ice cream, all paying homage to the magnificent Knickerbocker Glories. It had a wonderful jukebox, which attracted me there when I was a reporter in an office up the road in Hamilton Street. In those days in the 1960s, we would have Titanic-sinking lunches, listening to rock and roll songs, while the old ladies filed in to play bingo in the upstairs hall. It is all gone now.

Despite their rivalries, which were more keenly felt by the civic elders than the ordinary people, Birkenhead and Liverpool were joined by a railway tunnel in 1886. It ran from Liverpool James Street to Green Lane, Birkenhead, opposite the gates to the shipyard. Two years later a branch line was opened between Hamilton Square and Birkenhead Park. This drastically reduced the number of commuters taking the ferries between the Liverpool Pier Head and Birkenhead's Woodside jetty, near the original landing stage by the priory.

The lift juddered and complained as it sank to the underground platform carrying Tom, me and a few disconsolate commuters. The train to Liverpool hummed along, fast and soulless.

Sharp daylight greeted us at the exit of Moorfields station (1977), the newest on the system, serving the old part of the city. "I always think of the beautiful melody and poetic opening to George Harrison's *Here Comes the*

Sun when I step out of an underground station," I said to Tom. "For me it was the best of The Beatles' songs. Each time I hear it I feel an inner chill. I think of the first sun at the beginning of the world bringing light to all the people, like God."

"It's strange how a simple sentiment could mean so much," he said, as we walked towards the marble café at a corner of Old Hall Street, probably the windiest street in the world.

"Ah well, George was a complicated soul," I said. "Although I never met him, he was the Beatle I identified with most. One day, when I was about 14, I was walking along a suburban road with some friends talking about The Beatles. We were saying all the usual things. You know, John Lennon was the intellectual one with the acerbic wit, the rebel with a love of rock and roll; Paul McCartney was the melody man, who had a love of the big American shows and the British music hall tradition, the cherub-faced chap, who would appeal to mum, though he was really a randy fellow, whose disarming grin should have been a warning to lock-up your daughters; and Ringo Starr was the joker, who had a keen intelligence and a deep understanding of human nature behind his heavy-lidded eyes.

"What about George?" I asked the others. He was the 'looker' they said. All the girls fancied him.

"Of course," I continued, "we were to learn later in his life that there was a lot more to him. He was a spiritual man, who had a keen nose for money. Yes, there were contradictions. His ancestry was Irish and he had that sort of beguiling face, but in many ways he was very English, loving the native eccentricity as represented by the Monty Python TV comedy team, the antics of George Formby and his famous ukulele, Ealing comedies and other English films. He was very witty, making mordant observations on life, which easily matched those of John. But George will be remembered as the spiritual Beatle, the one most willing to try other religions in the vain hope of uncovering the meaning of life."

Tom, whose grand statue of John as the self-willed rebel stands at Liverpool Airport, seemed to concur with at least some of my assessment.

I had covered the death of George for the *Liverpool Daily Post* on November 29, 2001. Most of what you write for newspapers is forgotten in the whirl of the world. If the words live at all, they are in the sleeping hollows of the archive. But there was a quality in George that had deeply appealed to me – the spiritual man trapped in a material world, accepting fame but reaching for anonymity at the same time. In this way, he became a bruised messiah. So what came out? This is what I remember writing on that sad day.

"Lovers and losers, the mighty and poor of the world, were yesterday listening to the songs of the bus driver's son, who gave everyone a memory, a time to smile. That was his gift to us."

"The man you're about to meet is a great fan of George's," said Tom – and there sitting at a table in a dip of the café, where the band used to play, was Anthony (Tony) Brown, blue-eyed, smiling, and fair-haired, a goatee beard beginning to sprout on his chin in the artistic style. Tony painted portraits of distinguished people for his '100 Heads Thinking as One' exhibition of 2007 to celebrate the 800th anniversary of King John granting Liverpool the Royal Charter, officially recognising its status as an English port, but more of that later.

Tony Brown studies faces for his exhibition

Tony Brown at work

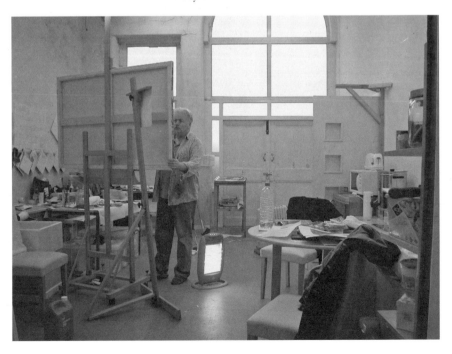

It had been Tony's original idea to feature only living Liverpudlians, but, in this city of immortality, it became necessary to extend the project to include a few distinguished dead people. That number had to include John Lennon and George Harrison. Behind these portraits, Tony had blended images from the lives of his subjects – smaller pictures of people and places from their past and present, newspaper cuttings and much-favoured objects. In this way, each portrait became a biography. Earlier in his career, Tony had painted a more conventional portrait of Brian Epstein, The Beatles' manager. In 1999, he had offered the painting to the Neptune Theatre in Hanover Street, Liverpool, where it was hung in the bar.

Tony, his half-smile gently exercised, assumed mastery of the swollen china pot, in which the tea had been slowly maturing. When the moment was ripe, he raised the steaming pot from a cork mat on the altar-white table-cloth and tilted it over each cup, watching the tea pour from the spout, as dark as a ghost's soul, coffin-brown, just the way I like it.

Tony's portraits have been shown in the neo-classical splendour of St George's Hall, as well as Liverpool's Anglican Cathedral and the Roman Catholic Metropolitan Cathedral of Christ the King, less grandly known

100 Heads in St George's Hall

Great Liverpudlians – Tony Brown, Michael Kelly and Ron Formby

as Paddy's Wigwam. His "doodle" line drawings of the Liverpool and New York waterfronts adorn T-shirts, posters, training shoes, mugs and plates on both sides of the Atlantic.

"But I know Tony," I said to Tom, as I adjusted to the surroundings. "I didn't realise he was the man you were talking about. I've known him for years. He's an old friend."

"Yes, I wondered if you did," said Tom. "Even so, I thought it would be nice for the three of us could have a cuppa together – particularly as you intend writing about Great Liverpudlians and how paintings and statues can bestow a kind of immortality on the right people.

"If you are accepted and then loved in this city, you'll never be forgotten. You told me that once. I'm sure Tony agrees."

"I do," he said.

"But I don't just see John as a Beatle," he added. "In him, I found the essence of Liverpool. He had that swagger. And you can see that in Tom's statue. There was a generosity of spirit in him, but there were also flashes of cruelty. All that's in the changing expression of his face. He had the big smile, but he also had the severity, a withering look, which was almost schoolmasterly. He was a genius. You can hear that in the deceptively simple melodies, carrying deeply felt sentiments such as in his song, *There Are Places I Remember*."

"Some critics condemned *Imagine* as a secular hymn lacking any real point," I said, "but I think it scores because of its simplicity. The sentiment is not original – the notion that possessions and property are the barriers to peace and goodwill has been held by many down the ages, but the tune is very strong. Expressing so much in such a simple way requires genius. Great tomes have been written on the same subjects. You read them and end up knowing less. All the great spiritual utterances are poetic and simple, just caressing the inner beliefs that people already have. The point is that he did it. *Imagine* is not a drippy-hippie song, it's actually very direct. You know, being rich is not always a barrier to understanding that greed is wrong.

"Although they were very different men, I sometimes think of Wilfred Owen, the Great War poet, when people are talking about Lennon. Perhaps that's because of Lennon's associations with the peace movement. Owen spent four years of his childhood in Birkenhead. He attended Bible classes at Christ Church, near my home in Oxton Village. Sometimes, when I was walking into town, I could visualise Wilfred as a 10-year-old boy, walking from his family's home in Tranmere, about a mile away. He was only 10 then, with a pale, round face, but I saw the yearning in his eyes, those eyes you might remember from books and magazines, usually carrying the caption, 'Wilfred Owen: War Poet', accompanied by his famous statement of purpose, 'My subject is war and the pity of war. The poetry is in the pity'."

Tom Murphy, the sculptor, gives his subjects a kind of immortality

Tom Murphy's statues of Ken Dodd & Bessie Braddock arrives in Liverpool
– the right way up
© ANTHONY AND LORRAINE BROWN EMSO ARTS

But we had been talking about The Beatles, before I was diverted.

"Lennon's *Jealous Guy* is another lovely melody," I said. "However, I think it was Paul who had genius in the true sense of something coming to him without cultivation, a natural and inexplicable talent. He told us that *Yesterday*, not my favourite song of his but perhaps the most famous, came to him in a dream. That is genius. You have to differentiate that quality from a talent developed through practice."

The conversation drifted into the importance of The Beatles to Liverpool. There are some patriotic people in the city who think that it is too big, dwarfing Liverpool's other assets. They would like more attention to be drawn the buildings, theatres, museums and other places of learning, as well as the Victorian heritage of the city as the second port of the British Empire. But it could be that the four young Beatles carried the many qualities, which have helped Liverpool to stand apart from the rest of Britain – the Celtic passion, the knowing wit, the unyielding loyalty, the readiness to mock those who are different or strange, the natural suspicion, the total, absolute and utter dislike of authority. Brian Epstein (or "Epsteen", as it is pronounced in Liverpool) encountered this. He was a Jew at a time when racial intolerance was quite prevalent. More than that, however, he was evidently middle-class, the son of successful business people, and this could be heard in his accent and seen in his elegantly tailored suits and gentle manners, which immediately suggested homosexuality to the canny-eyed.

Perhaps nothing better exemplifies The Beatles' understanding of these things than their first meeting with him on November 9, 1961, in the cramped dressing-room at the Cavern Club on Mathew Street. "And what brings Mr Epstein here?" said George.

So much street wisdom is held in those few words.

"Do you think The Beatles would have made it without Epstein?" I asked. "When I was growing up, the conventional notion was that he made them. In a sense that reflects another age. It was widely assumed then that business acumen was more important than raw talent. To write songs and perform them was one thing, but to make money out of them was quite another."

"Yes," said Tony. "Epstein, or Eppy as local friends called him, was the right man to do that. He was a businessman but he was also a modern man, who seemed to have an instinctive understanding of the changes happening in post-war Britain. He wasn't particularly well educated by the measure of exams, despite the money his parents paid out, packing him off to boarding schools, but he had savvy. He would have had more in common with The Beatles than was at first apparent. True, his family was rich and wanted their son to have the polished manners of the upper middle-classes, but Paul, John and George had all been to grammar schools, which in those days aped the ways of the public schools. Because of the British obsession with class, writers on The Beatles have always sought to emphasise their differences rather than their similarities. At the core they were all rebels, who had arrived at just the right moment. George's introductory remark at the Cavern could be taken as almost prophetic."

I mentioned that in 1970, George Melly, had written a book called *Revolt into Style*, which told of how in the process of becoming famous, many rebels of the 1960s had been tamed. As a fine blues and jazz singer, a grand raconteur, art lover, an incorrigible gossip, and splendid writer, whose sexual appetites were as broad as his girth, Melly knew his subject. He was also another great Liverpudlian – a roly-poly package of generous humanity, permanently bursting at the seams.

In addition to being a cultural examination of the 1960s, "Gorgeous" Melly's book was making the point that under strict management the moody teenager, with greasy hair, leering slips and a guitar slung over his shoulders in the style of Elvis Presley, could be transformed into Buttons in time for the Christmas pantomime. That was the fate of many British pop stars of the era. That never happened to any of The Beatles.

"Epstein realised that he was dealing with true artists," said Tom. "He knew that they were different from some of the other people he managed, such as Cilla Black and Gerry (Marsden) and the Pacemakers.

"I don't think he was against summer shows and pantos. In fact, Cilla, particularly, became one of the country's finest all-round entertainers. From the start, Epstein saw that she could follow in the tradition of Gracie Fields.

Epstein must have had a real insight into The Beatles because there was a time early in their careers when it seemed they could have gone that way. They clowned about a bit on popular TV shows and were required to quip impishly, but they were soon regarded more seriously.

"To be honest in Liverpool, the newspapers and the more conventional mums and dads wanted them to remain forever the Fab Four, those lovable Mop Tops. The Liverpool establishment never really celebrated the long-haired, psychedelic Beatles. When they became thinkers, instead of puppets, it was almost seen as a betrayal here. Of course, in some ways that mirrors Britain as a whole. We like our stars to be stuck on the end of the pier, jokers rather than philosophers. Epstein, whose affection for The Beatles was emotional as well as intellectual, knew his boys were different, destined for a higher place in history."

"In the rebel pose, The Beatles are generally assumed to have taken their lead from Elvis and the American rock and rollers like Gene Vincent and Eddie Cochran," I said. "Buddy Holly was obviously another strong influence, but wasn't Lonnie Donegan more important to The Beatles and the general direction of British pop music?"

"Absolutely," replied Tony. "The skiffle craze in the 1950s changed everything. People totally underestimate the importance of Lonnie. The success of his records, starting with the Rock Island Line, persuaded thousands of young Britons to form skiffle groups. The Beatles, Gerry and the Pacemakers and nearly all the Merseybeat groups started as skifflers, playing American folk songs in the coffee bars and suburban cellars of the UK."

"If we accept that The Beatles were the greatest group it leaves open the question of who came second in that glorious decade of British pop and rock," I said, "In a sense the real competition was for second place. In asking the question, I was aware of the opinion offered by Dominic Sandbrook in *White Heat*, his masterful history of "the Swinging Sixties".

This is what he wrote: "Many beat groups subsided into obscurity after 1964, the turbulent tides of musical fashion having left them high and dry. The obvious exception, and by far the most talented of all The Beatles' rivals, was a group from north London, the Kinks … and more than any other group of the sixties they exemplified ways in which British pop music drew on domestic cultural traditions as well as on the often rather exaggerated influences of the United States."

It seems likely that some of the songs written by Ray Davies of the Kinks, such as *Waterloo Sunset*, *Sunny Afternoon*, *Dead End Street*, *Days*, *Come Dancing* and *Lola*, will be judged by history to be as least as good as the best of The Beatles. But the question I posed was for Liverpool only. Interestingly, Ray Davies, the Kinks' songwriter, had originally intended *Waterloo Sunset*, one of the finest songs English songs of the twentieth century, to be *Liverpool Sunset*, as a reflection that Merseybeat was fading in 1967, but as a Londoner he changed it to *Waterloo Sunset* and the "dirty old river" is the Thames and not the Mersey.

"To me it's The Searchers," I said. "They were the second group in Liverpool. Their version of *Needles and Pins* is one of the finest pop singles ever recorded. The influence of the astonishing vocal harmonies and the jingly-jangly guitars can be heard in later American groups such as the Byrds and the Eagles. Their legacy is immense."

Tom and Tony considered the question but gave no answers. It is a difficult question and it could be answered differently, according to your mood at the time. But you think of The Big Three, The Undertakers, The Remo Four, The Mojos, The Swinging Blue Jeans, The Escorts, The Merseybeats, Faron's Flamingos and so on and on. There were hundreds of good groups on Merseyside at the time. However, it has to be accepted that The Beatles stand alone.

"Obviously, Liverpool has great buildings, a fascinating history and wonderful people, but that is true of most cities. Look at any holiday brochure and you will see European cities with grand churches, cathedrals and public buildings. Tourists tick the boxes, press the buttons on their cameras and move on. Some people may not like me saying this, but it is largely through The Beatles that we have remained one of the world's great cities, known everywhere," added Tom, after a pause.

"I think the future of the city will depend to a large extent on their reputation being sustained. I think it will. The Beatles are forever like the great classical composers and musicians. History is a tight, selective procedure. Once you are in it, you tend to stay there. The Beatles have their place. It is a simple as that."

"When I was young, my parents generation would have scoffed at the notion of The Beatles being compared to Mozart and Beethoven. The Beatles themselves would have laughed at them then," I said. "You know, one day I was talking to a woman, who was quite elderly, and she told me that she had been listening to all The Beatles' number one records in her car. She described it as "a sublime hour".

Tony reached for the pot. Refills were needed. The time had come to look back, long before the age of our bruised messiahs.

3

OF CASTLES, DOCKS, PRIESTS & SUGAR

THE MORNING BROODED and weary moments passed through the juddering fingers on the clock above our table. A man with the blue eyes of a philosopher was sitting at the next table, guiding his fork towards the saddle on a plump pork sausage, which he then stabbed with a single thrust. Flavoursome juice spurted from the four-pronged wound.

This was Ron Formby, observer of life and then the angular editor of the *Scottie Press*, the community newspaper serving the Vauxhall neighbourhood of the city, including the famous Scotland Road, once celebrated for having a pub on every corner.

The gleaming black shoes of priests, many still yearning for the peat fires of their native Ireland, strode the chattering streets of the impoverished parishes, overlooked by grandiose brick churches with gulls perching on the high crosses. These priests remembered the names of all the hungry children, while grinning, pale-moon faced, into the prayers of the mothers in those silent hours of darkness, which belonged to God – before the bicycle bells of the early workers rang out the new day.

In this neighbourhood, many Irish people had settled after fleeing the Potato Famine of the 1840s. It was a holy place of suffering and laughter, one squeezing the hand of the other. People experienced the extremes of life and conducted themselves accordingly, while forming one of the strongest communities in Europe.

Immigrants from Italy, Lithuania, Germany, Greece, Scandinavia and many countries came here. Some were hoping for a new life in the USA, others stayed in Liverpool.

Many of the priests were fine and noble with a simple basic faith; others had doubts and desires, which could be soothed or stirred in the long and lonely nights of drink and prayer. They were just men with all the strengths and weaknesses given by God. In those days their influence on the community was immeasurable.

But if you mention the name of Father Godfrey Carney to the old people, who remember him and his devotion, you will hear only words of respect.

Those were the days when the trees in distant lands hung heavy with fruits to be picked and loaded on the ships heading for Liverpool. And in the sheds along foreign shores, rotund merchants in brilliant clothes sprinkled spices into drums. Fabrics, exotic perfumes and molasses came into our port. Tools, heavy machines and sweat went out. Cranes groaned. Ropes strained. Cigarettes were rolled. Mugs of tea were drained. Brows were mopped on shirtsleeves, as the sun, which warmed an empire, crept over the Mersey docks. Fathers and sons humped sacks along the quays and the hardened fingers of the passing generations joined Liverpool to Asia, America, Europe, Africa and Australasia.

Dockers were at the heart of Liverpool, with their alehouses and tall stories, the nicknames and the humour, their politics, a sense of street justice, strong family bonds, natural cunning, and a refusal to bow to authority.

Men had been loading and unloading boats on both sides of the river for centuries. The Benedictine monks in Birkenhead were, in a way, the first dockers. Early trading was mainly with Ireland. Most of us have those photographs of the memory, showing how the docks looked with the cranes and capstans and deep stonewalls.

Before that, however, small boats would rest on the mud when the tide went out. They would be unloaded before it came in again. Larger ships could be damaged when they ran aground, so they anchored in the river and fleets of smaller craft carried the cargoes to and from them. By the 1660s, ships were travelling to North America to trade in sugar, tobacco, cloth, pottery and other goods. As the trading grew, it became obvious that we needed a system to cope. The solution was docks, walled-in areas, where the level of water could be maintained. Thomas Steers, the civil engineer, built the world's first enclosed wet basin in 1715 in what is now Canning Place. In 1826, it was filled-in to become the site of the Custom House.

More docks were built along the fronts at Liverpool, Bootle, Seaforth, Birkenhead and Wallasey. Among them were Canning (1737–1972), Salthouse (1773–1952), Georges (1771–1899), Dukes (1773–1972) Kings (1785–1972) and Coburg (1796–1972). The great Victorian docks included the Albert, Alexandra, Brocklebank, Brunswick, Canada, Clarence, Herculaneum, Hornby, Huskisson, Langton, Princes, Sandon, Stanley, Trafalgar, Victoria Wapping, Waterloo, Morpeth, Egerton, Wallasey, Alfred, the Great Float, Vittoria and Bidston.

View across the Mersey

© AUTHOR

Although to some historians, Liverpool grew into the Celtic city planted in England, and thus a place apart, a glance through those names tell us that the business community at least celebrated the Royal Family and the British Empire. In 1880 Liverpool had been granted city status.

But working conditions were poor. The men were treated as casual labourers hired on a daily or on a weekly basis. There were regular strikes and lockouts. In 1947, the National Dock Labour Board introduced a register, which gave the job greater stability.

"Casualisation", which left men not knowing if they would work or not, ended altogether after a strike in 1967. From then on the working hours of dockers were guaranteed. This led to a period of comparative affluence on the Mersey.

But times were changing and the UK's entry into the Common Market (EU) in the early 1970s changed the country's trading patterns from the old Empire to Europe. At its peak in the 1950s, the port had employed about 25,000 dockers. As we entered the new century, the number had fallen to 400, most of those at the Seaforth container terminal. In 1995 there had been a final rising of the old ways, when men were loyal to each other and their faith. Some 325 dockers at Seaforth were sacked for refusing to cross the picket line of striking workers from a stevedoring company. The strike/lock-out was long and bitter, stirring sympathy among the much-depleted Socialist groups of the area and elsewhere. The men from the Transport and General Workers Union held out for 850 days, demanding their reinstatement. In the end, though, most of them accepted pay-offs, which had increased during the dispute.

These were the changing times for Father Carney, rangy of build with a gentle manner, who first offered his heart to Liverpool in 1934, when the faith was strong but tummies were empty. The General Strike of 1926 had left a sense of bitterness in the working-class communities and the "Hungry Thirties" aggravated this.

Mussolini was posturing in Italy. Hitler was making his plans in Germany and mesmerising mass gatherings. Ironically it would be our war against those dictators which would revive patriotism in the communities that had been given such a raw deal by those in charge in London.

Father Carney's first posting was at St Sylvester's Church, off old Scottie Road. I didn't know him until he was an old man, but we became friends and I could visualise how he had been, thanks in part to his own wonderful powers of description.

He was a fine and noble figure, who smiled at life in the most sympathetic way through the slow blue of his eyes, shaking his head at the crazy parade, but always marvelling at how, amid the confusion and sorrow, there arose poems and melodies, grand sculptures, paintings and the ceaseless beat of the human spirit.

He was an old country apple of a chap – the skin was rough and bruised here and there, but inside the juice was sweet and good. His belief in God thundered within, but it was never expressed loudly. In noise lay emptiness, in the silence came reason. He died in 2008 and I often wonder now if he found everything he wanted.

Is it just as he was told it would be when he was a boy in the family farm in Crossboy, County Sligo, where, by the sighs of a turf fire, his lovely mother Ellen would read to him from the Bible and classical literature?

The wisdom, which had come naturally to Father Carney, was polished at All Hallows College, Dublin, where he trained for the priesthood. He served several parishes, mostly on Merseyside, before returning to near his old patch in 1978, as the resident priest at St John's Church, Kirkdale. He worked there until two years before his death.

One day, towards the end, I was talking to him about Sir Percy French, the Irish songwriter and entertainer. Well, Godfrey Carney had done some writing himself, occasionally aided by a wee whiskey and ginger, holding the tumbler in his great-knuckled hand.

"Ah Percy French," he said and then, in a voice pitched between tenor and baritone, he began singing: Oh, Mary, this London's a wonderful sight, with people all working by day and by night. Sure they don't sow potatoes, nor barley, not wheat, but there's gangs of them digging for gold in the street."

Yes, *The Mountains of Mourne* had been the lament of the homesick colleens and their young men, but by the time of Father Carney's going, the Liverpool Irish were as English as anyone else, except, perhaps on St Patrick's Day.

Sometimes, though, when the cats of the night prowl the alleys, I see a tall man lift the receiver on a black phone in the priest house. "Yes, Father Carney speaking. Gravely ill, you say. To be sure, I'll be there directly. Now, don't you be worrying. You've done all a woman could do, but he still needs you by him. I'm on my way."

It was the sense of a community, often held by religious faith, surviving through adversity that appeals so much to Ron, who believes it offers an example to the whole world. He looked over to Tom, Tony and me, after skinning the tomato on his plate with the skill of a surgeon removing a cataract. We all know each other.

Each month Ron's paper had carried stories and photographs of Scotland Road in the old days, when men of all shapes and sizes handled cargoes from all over the world along the quaysides, so that they could put a little food on their own tables.

Everyone knew Scotland Road then – the 1,640 yards stretching from Scotland Place to Boundary Street. In the 1330s, a white Cross had been laid as a marker on a spot near the present Hopwood Street. The track leading north, the ancient route to Scotland, became a turnpike road and it was widened in 1803, the true beginning of the road, which is so celebrated in Liverpool folklore.

The Christian tradition of learning meant that most of the schools offered a good if sometimes harsh education – the classics often came with the keen cut of the cane. But this meant that a steady number of boys and girls left the area and entered the professions. Many big families were proud to offer Holy Church a nun, a priest, or both. The factories, the shops and the docks provided work for those who remained.

In the 1960s and '70s, the municipal planners bulldozed the old streets and families moved to the new estates. It was a different Liverpool. Everyone had baths with running water, TVs, fridges, electric cookers and automatic washing machines. There was enough food to go round.

This was what everyone had prayed for, their nicotine-stained fingers grasping stubby pencils to scrape the names of doomed horses on scraps of papers in the bookie's shop – or crossing themselves before crossing the pools' coupons of Littlewoods or Vernons, both based in Liverpool, who had together turned the Saturday night reading of the football results into a sacred ritual.

The improvements had come with the economic recovery, which spread though the country after the long post-war years of austerity. But, as is so often the case, material advantage had left a spiritual hole. People were less neighbourly in the new houses. Doors were closed at night and curtains drawn. The televisions flickered like magic lanterns, drawing all eyes into them. Something had been lost. The old communities bonded on adversity had gone to be replaced by a tawdry, superficial affluence that had done nothing to break down the old class barriers. It had merely moved them.

If Ron had a mission in life it was to ensure that the coming generations never forget how it had been. In addition the docks and the church, the old community had been together held by commerce and industry, particularly sugar.

Sugar meant Tate & Lyle in Liverpool. Old-timers remember those mornings of jangling keys when down the streets, arm-in-arm, gossiped the girls in blue and white checked turbans. Some still had toast crumbs on their lips, as they stepped to work in the lamp-lit dawn. The bicycle bells rang from one to the other over the bridges crossing the Leeds and Liverpool Canal.

Sugar had pleased ancient palates, but its popularity really grew with the colonisation of West Indian Islands by the Spanish, British and French. Huge plantations spread across the Caribbean in the eighteenth, nineteenth and twentieth centuries.

Vast numbers of slaves were used to cut the cane shipped to European ports. Slavery was abolished in the British Empire in 1833, but for many Africans the conditions on the plantations remained grim.

In practice, you had black men cutting the cane with machetes for white men and women. From this, brown sugar or molasses was processed. But it could be further refined into white sugar for those of particularly delicate taste.

This was the main purpose of the factory opened in 1872 by the businessman Henry Tate on the Leeds and Liverpool Canal in Vauxhall. The sugar was also cut into little squares, associated with the cartoon character Mr Cube, drawn by Bobby St John Cooper, and introduced to sugar bags in 1949.

Working in the factory was hard and the profits were high for the bosses and shareholders, but Tate, a philanthropist and champion of the arts, established a regime of good and fair labour relations, which would sustain almost to the end. In 1921, his company merged with the Lyle group, particularly famed for its syrup. The Scottish businessman Abram Lyle had started it.

Tate & Lyle, with more than 3,000 on the pay roll at its peak, was the biggest employer in the area, apart from the docks.

Despite the disapproval of the authorities, children swam in the canal along a stretch called the "Scaldies", where boiling water was discharged from the refining process. Pale children with ribs like banjo strings shuddered as they slipped into the water, clinging to their "cossies" in case anyone could see the secret bits. Gulls whistled in the sky.

However, there was never a strike at the refinery where goodwill generally prevailed. When it was recommended that it should close in 1971, such was the public outcry that the company decided to continue.

Tate & Lyle, which then employed 2,000 people in this factory on the quaintly named Love Lane, was still a good employer, providing its staff with sports facilities and a social clubs. The company turbans provided safety and hygiene and the "girls" wore them with pride. Retired sugar workers also looked forward to the Tate & Lyle Christmas hampers, which would be delivered to their homes. On Friday nights they would go the Goat pub. A group called the Gin Bottle Four entertained the regulars in the concert room, but, as the night matured, sometimes the Gin Bottle Four would be joined on stage by enthusiasts, becoming the Gin Bottle Five, Six and so on.

However, even a benevolent company had to face facts. There was surplus capacity caused by Europe's Common Agricultural Policy, which heavily subsidised the rival sugar beet – leading to the slogan, "keep the cane and beat the beet".

In 1981, the refinery finally closed with the direct loss of 1,570 jobs with hundreds more in dependent commerce and industry losing their jobs.

These were the dark days in Liverpool, superbly and sympathetically chronicled by Alan Bleasdale in his TV series *Boys from the Black Stuff*, with part of an episode filmed in the Green Man pub, opposite the old refinery.

Like Charles Dickens a century earlier, Bleasdale held the nation in thrall. Dickens's novels had appeared in instalments in magazines. Bleasdale's stories were shown in weekly episodes. Meanwhile, the Anglican Bishop of Liverpool, the Right Reverend David Sheppard, and the Roman Catholic Archbishop, the Most Reverend Derek Worlock, had helped form the Congress of Merseyside, a campaigning body comprising other clergymen and politicians determined to protect Merseyside from economic disaster.

At the end of 1981, the Government's attention was drawn to Liverpool by major disturbances in another part of the city, the more racially mixed Toxteth. The "Toxteth Riots", accompanied by similar troubles elsewhere in the UK, prompted Prime Minister Margaret Thatcher to make Michael Heseltine, a more liberal figure on the old Tory tradition, her special minister for Merseyside, as part of his wider responsibilities as Secretary of State for the Environment.

Thanks in part to the energy of Heseltine, conditions gradually improved. Heseltine, with his flowing golden locks and handsome appearance, was dubbed "Tarzan" by the Press. His greatest achievement on Merseyside was the International Garden Festival, which ran in Liverpool from May to October 1984. Although its legacy was disappointing until new plans were announced for the site in 2010, it did bring in big crowds – reminding people that Liverpool had more to offer than football, pop music, comedians and a peculiar pride that didn't seem entirely British.

But the community spirit hadn't completely died. After long negotiations, involving Bishop Sheppard, Archbishop Worlock and even Prince Charles, local activists, led by Tony McGann, secured a £6.4m grant to start building the Eldonian Village on the refinery site.

By 1989, 145 dwellings had been built, followed by another 150 houses. Today, it remains a model village with its individually designed houses, gardens, a community hall and other facilities, as well as the canal running through it. This is a supreme example of how the community spirit can still operate in the modern world.

So there we were – Tony, Tom, Ron and myself in the café on Old Hall Street. Sadly, few of those passing by our window would have known that this building was in the heart of old Liverpool, the ancient port.

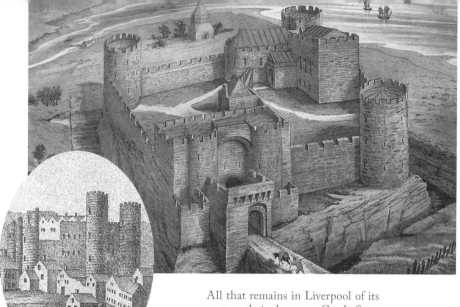

All that remains in Liverpool of its
great castle is the name Castle Street

On August 28, 1207, in Winchester, King John had issued a Letters Patent (popularly known as the Royal Charter), which established Liverpool as a port.

A Letters Patent is an open document issued by a monarch or government, which grants an office, a right, a monopoly, a title or status to an individual or group. John had obtained the fishing hamlet of Liverpool from the Norman landowner, Henry Fitzwarin, in exchange for other land. The idea was for people to settle on burgages (plots of land). The tenants had to pay a shilling a year for each plot to the king, who wanted an embarkation point for his fleet, so that soldiers could be sent to deal with any rebellions that might break out in disputatious Ireland, over which England had claimed sovereignty. It was also thought that a castle would add substance to these ambitions, while providing accommodation for the troops.

Work on the castle had begun before John's death in 1216. It has been suggested that a small fort already stood on the site. John, of course, gives Liverpool what modern politicians and publicists would call "an image problem".

Yes, he was the father of the port, but he is generally regarded in history as an ignominious scoundrel, a reputation darkened still more by his role as the bad egg in the entirely fictitious tales of Robin Hood. School children in the past had been introduced to John in *1066 and All That* (1930), a sparkling spoof history of England written by the magnificently named Walter Carruthers Sellar and Robert Julian Yeatman.

When John lost his temper, they wrote, he "flung himself on the floor, foaming at the mouth and biting rushes".

Perhaps he realised that such displays of pique could not be tolerated in Liverpool, where people are expected to suffer life's mishaps with a resigned shrug or a bleak joke. Anyway, there's not much that can be done about him now, though a canny PR, charged with selling him to the public, might try and present him as an enthusiast kicker of the inflated pig's bladder, before the innocent pleasures of football were corrupted by money.

Maybe he could also be depicted as a bearded hippie with a benign smile, plucking his lyre while singing, "Yesterday, all my troubles seemed so far away …"

The original plan of Liverpool, designed by his agents, was an H-shape of seven streets. These were Castle Street, Dale Street, Bank (now Water) Street, Juggler (High) Street, Chapel Street, Moor Street and Whiteacre (Old Hall) Street.

The Victoria Monument on Derby Square would have been in the middle of the castle, which had a main entrance in a wall of some 36 yards, facing what is now Castle Street. The building was on a constructed plateau over a moat cut from solid rock. It was a formidable presence with a gatehouse flanked by two towers at the north-east corner facing Castle Street. Three towers dominated the other corners. The thick sandstone walls were hewn from local quarries. It was an excellent defensive position, surrounded on three sides by water, which, according to contemporary sources, was not "a bow's shot away". The castle had its own bakery, brewery and chapel.

The old saying "out of sight, out of mind" has application here. The castle can't be seen now, so its part in Liverpool's history has been largely forgotten. We should, though, remember that the castle stood for some 500 years – far longer than the totemic Royal Liver Building, the cathedrals or the football stadiums.

Its end started in the English Civil War. Most Liverpudlians ("Liverpolitans" is still favoured by

Flattering images of King John – father of all the Scousers

some) had sided with Oliver Cromwell and the Parliamentarians, though thin-lipped puritanism had never been the style of the port. But preparations were made to defend Liverpool against an expected attack from Prince Rupert, the nephew of Charles I, whose feuds with Parliament had led to the war.

Rupert was the dashing cavalier of the popular imagination, a fine if reckless cavalry officer, who had fought on the battlefields of Europe. Cannons were strategically placed, ramparts were built and a ditch was dug, 12 yards wide and nine feet deep, but it was not enough.

In June 1644, Rupert and his army arrived at a rise, on the site of the present Lime Street railway station. From there, they bombarded the castle and then, on June 10, they made a flank attack in the direction of Old Hall Street, where we were drinking tea. Rupert and his men fought their way to the castle gates. A truce was arranged and the town surrendered to the King's cause.

Sir John Moore later regained it for Cromwell and the Parliamentarians. The permanent population of Liverpool then was little more than 1,000, many of whom died in the fighting and hardship that resulted from it.

Soon after the restoration in 1660, Charles II had the garrison removed and the castle partly dismantled. However, the soldiers of William III used it during an Irish campaign in 1688. By 1770 it had become a shelter for the homeless and 14 years later George I authorised its removal. The site was given to the Mayor and Corporation of Liverpool at an annual rent of £6 13s and 4d (£6.67). St George's Church was built there and then rebuilt before work began on the Victoria monument in 1902.

But it is not completely lost to our sight. Enter William Hesketh Lever, the soap magnate and first Lord Leverhulme, who built Port Sunlight village for his workers on the banks of the Mersey, near Birkenhead.

He became fascinated by the castle and ordered a replica to be built on his estate at Rivington, near Bolton. But this would not be a model in all its glory with knights in shining armour, goblets of mead, and maidens in distress. His idea was to recreate the castle as it had been after the Civil War. He was, in fact, building a ruin, "Leverhulme's Folly".

He called it "an experiment in landscape design". Work on it began in 1912, but it hadn't finished when he died in 1925. Tourists still visit the "new" ruin, which, of course, is growing old in its own right.

The waterfront area of Liverpool looked entirely different then, much of it being under the pool (or inlet) from which the city gets its name. The Mersey and numerous little streams rushed down from the higher ground, feeding the pool, which occupied the area now embracing Pembroke Place, London Road, Stafford Street, Islington, Christian Street, the old Haymarket, Whitechapel and Paradise Street. Between the 1670s and the middle of the next century, the pool was filled-in by docks and other developments, becoming the landscape familiar today.

Leverhulme's Folly at Rivington
© BOLTON EVENING NEWS

But before that could happen, Liverpool was shaken by one of the most important events in its early history.

Stretch your imagination back to 1669. Smoke plumes from the chimneys of squat stone and timber cottages. Gulls swoop and hens scratch. Steamed breath shudders from the great heads of horses. The old pool was more than a geographical dividing line.

One side was comparatively prosperous. It contained the seven original streets. In addition to paying rent to the monarch, the early settlers collected ferry tolls and had begun small businesses. After John's death, his impecunious successor, Henry III, sold Liverpool to the Earl of Chester. Over the next 400 years the port had several different landlords, all of whom received money for it.

By 1632 Lord Molyneux and his family had acquired all rights to the growing town, but as supporters of the Royalists in the Civil War, they laid low for a while on their estate in Croxteth. However, with the easing of tensions, Caryll Molyneux had ordered the construction of Lord Molyneux Street from the castle's orchard to what is now Lord Street on the edge of the pool. Then, in 1669, he decided to build a bridge linking his land to the other side, a sparsely populated spread, which the people believed to be held in common ownership.

Molyneux's purpose was to develop this land for his own commercial advantage, extending it up the hill to what became Bold Street. Now, perhaps for the first time in the story, we have a sense of the defiant mood, which would become such a feature of the Liverpool character, the "Scouse spirit".

Two local protestors, supported by their fellows, demolished the bridge. You can almost see the firm jaw and steady Scouse stare of these two men taking their bow in history. Their names are recorded as Edward Marsh and James Whitfield.

But they were cunning as well as brave, realising that Molyneux may have made an error in his construction of the bridge. Some of the stones and rocks used to build it had come from their side of the pool. This was a fair point, which could be raised in any argument that might ensue.

Molyneux had Marsh and Whitfield were imprisoned, but their followers bailed them out and appointed solicitors to state their case.

On March 20, 1672, the Molyneux family settled out or court and agreed that the people in the settled area should have ownership of the land and its fees as well as access to the common land across the pool. Modern Liverpool was born.

Nine years later, work began on the first dock under the supervision of engineer Thomas Steers. By then there were some 40 streets in Liverpool and the population had grown to more than 7,000. The streams, which fed the old pool, would be directed into culverts.

"You know," said Ron, dabbing his lips with a napkin, "local people still call Liverpool the Pool."

"Yes, when I was a young man of ambition in Birkenhead, people would talk about going to the Pool" I replied. "That was the word they used and everyone understood it. You know everyone in this strange and wonderful city has a story to tell, but we will only have time to hear a few."

"Such is life," said Ron. "You would need all the time in the world to hear all the stories."

In the late 1980s, Ron had joined the Vauxhall Neighbourhood Council, the community-based organisation and publisher of the *Scottie Press*. Dealings with what he would called "quangoesque" organisations, which take "three conferences, six meetings, five seminars and an away day" to prepare the menu for their next lunch, had filled his immense intellect with a true evaluation of British life.

In 2009, the *Daily Telegraph* published a series of revelations about what MPs had been claiming on their expenses. Among those explaining embarrassing items on their lists was Alistair Darling, then the dark-browed, albino-haired Chancellor of the Exchequer. "He's in charge of our money, isn't he?" said Ron, when the news broke. "You couldn't make it up."

In a few words, Ron had made the most incisive observation about a national crisis.

4

A BLACK FACE AMONG THE RAGAMUFFINS

IT WAS TIME TO LEAVE THE CAFÉ, but the conversation was easy and all Liverpudlians love a good gab.

"Another pot of tea?" I suggested.

"Well, all life is just a work in progress, so why not?" said Tom.

"Very profound," said Tony, half smiling and as quiet as a shadow, in the way of a cool man, who appreciates art and music and life.

"If everyone spent their lives drinking tea, where would we all be?" asked Ron.

"Perhaps a bit happier than we are now," I replied.

"Oh God," said Ron, a master of observational humour, "not more Christmas-cracker philosophy from you. In an earlier life, you must have been one of those witch-doctors, who searched for the meaning of life in the entrails of chickens."

"Thank you for that," I said. "But I have a story to tell you about a Great Liverpudlian and this one is really fascinating."

"Go on then," said Ron, "but cut the flannel. Time is a tyrant and I'll have to be pushing along soon. Anyway, I know what your stories are like. You're not a man to use one word if 93 will do. We'll be neck-deep in adjectives before the tea is brewed."

"I think I'll have a nice hot-buttered scone with my tea," said Tony, who likes his food as an aid to concentration.

"The story begins in Jamaica back in the 1860s," I began.

"Well, it makes a change from Birkenhead in the 1960s," said Ron, who has a permanently simmering sense of humour, as well as an extraordinary capacity to assess a situation quickly. But I was determined to proceed.

"In 1833 slavery had been abolished in the British colonies. The slave owners were handsomely compensated and conditions for some of the black people improved, thanks in part to the intervention of missionaries, who had helped establish small plantations for them to run. The term "Negro peasant" fell into common usage then to explain their new status. Despite these improvements, though, the white plantation owners were still very much in charge. Some remained brutal in their treatment of black labour. Others were decent by the standards of the time. To confuse matters still more, many of the labourers were of mixed race, invariably having black mothers and white fathers for reasons that are all too obvious."

At this juncture in the story, Tony, Tom and Ron had no idea that it would lead all the way from the Caribbean islands to the famous Steble Fountain on William Brown Street, in the cultural heart of Liverpool – near the Walker Art Gallery, the World Museum, the Central Library and the neo-classical pillars of St George's Hall (the city's grandest building completed in the 1850s).

The fountain was erected in 1877 from an original design by Paul Lienard. Colonel RF Steble, Mayor of Liverpool in 1874–75, donated it to the city. The circular stone basin has a cast iron centrepiece with marine figures reclining beneath two smaller basins from which water tumbles out of a mermaid's shell and fish masks.

I could tell that my friends were listening keenly to this story, so I continued.

"Many of the labourers had been to mission schools. They had heard about people, whose lives were free from back-stooping toil and early death, while some of the people of mixed blood had reached positions of local prominence. As this was happening, economic conditions on the island started to worsen because of a collapse in the market for sugar coupled with rising taxes. Hunger and disease spread.

"The black community of Jamaica had never been passive for long. The history of the island had been scarred by bloody rebellions and then even bloodier repression. In theory the need for these uprisings should have ended in 1833 with the abolition of slavery, but comparatively little had really changed in the relations between the former slaves and their masters. For example in the 1860s, one man had been sentenced to 60 days hard labour for stealing a piece of cane worth threepence. Another was given 90 days hard labour for stealing rope.

"Educated black men began plotting the overthrow of their masters. Secret negotiations were held between the workers on different plantations.

"One of the men fomenting insurrection was George William Gordon (1820–65), the son of a plantation boss and a slave woman. He had broken the shackles of convention by becoming a landowner, a foaming evangelical preacher and a politician, who had even spoken for the oppressed in the

The black boy on the left of this photograph of the Steble fountain is William Masters,
who became the jazz musician Gordon Stretton

Jamaican Assembly. A sullen mood spread across the land. Almost inevitably, the hungry, black labourers rose-up, fired by passages in the Bible and notions of liberation. Had not Moses led his people out of bondage? 'Set my people free', was the fervent plea.

"It is interesting that the bloody events that followed are known to history as the Morant Bay "Slave Revolt" of 1865, though, as we have already noted, slavery had officially ended.

"Twenty whites and their followers were shot or hacked to death with the machetes that the labourers normally used for cutting cane. This provoked a furious response in which the better trained white troops killed 439 blacks and had some 600 flogged by "cats" whose nine tails had been reinforced with wire. There were trials of dubious legality and 354 rebels were strung up. Among them was Gordon, who became a national hero as a result.

"Soon black families were naming their children after him. Such had been the case with William Gordon Masters, the son of a slave, who left Jamaica to become a seaman. By quirk of fate, Masters was a familiar surname among the white families, whose slaves were frequently named after them to indicate ownership. Anyway, William Gordon Masters found freedom as a sailor and in the 1880s he met Ann Jane Williams, an Irish girl, who had settled near here, in Vauxhall. They married and had three sons. One was born in 1887 and was also named William Gordon Masters."

We paused while a waitress of nimble step brought a tray of tea and scones to our table.

"You know, there is a very famous photograph of the Steble Fountain," I went on. "It shows a dozen or so bare-footed ragamuffins. The photographer, Charles Frederick Inston, took it in 1890. There is one black face in the smiling group. Subsequent investigations, comparing the photograph to later ones, have proved that the black face belonged to William Gordon Masters junior.

"Although Liverpool was by then a cosmopolitan port, it was quite rare to see black people in some areas. They had not been integrated into the main community, though black seamen had been coming to Liverpool for centuries. A few had settled here, starting a small community, which grew after the American War of Independence (1775–81).

"George III had promised freedom to the black slaves if they served in our army. When the war was lost, many of them decided to leave America, arriving here in their uniforms. Some moved to the Toxteth district, joining the black seafarers, who were already living there. This gradually developed into a mixed race community with its own customs.

"Liverpool had prospered from the slave trade. European goods would be carried on ships to Africa, where they were bartered for slaves. Men, women and children were then carried in shameful conditions to the Caribbean islands and the USA. Hundreds of thousands died, stacked together in stinking holds as a human cargo. Slaves were not sold in Liverpool, but the ships' officers sometimes brought back black children and favoured women.

"Anyway, as I said, that black boy in the photograph, who seemed to be mixing very happily with all the others, was born and brought up off Scotland Road, where there were very few black residents. The area had absorbed people from Europe, but not Africa. So William must have been conscious of being different. Maybe that difference helped fire his ambition. For he became a star of music hall, a composer, a poet and a renowned jazz musician, using the name Gordon Stretton. He was a fine man with an immense international reputation, who is comparatively little known in his native city."

But before telling of his fame, we should divert briefly from the main narrative to follow another little story, which tell us so much about the times and circumstances of such Jamaican families. When he came to Liverpool, William's father carried with him a 600-page book called the *Christian Treasury*. It had been issued in instalments, which were then bound in leather into the full volume.

The editor was Horatius Bonar (1808–1889), a Scottish minister and hymnist, who became Moderator of the General Assembly of the Church of Scotland. His admirers knew him as the "prince" of Scottish hymns.

Among more than 600 offerings are *Angel Voices*; *Sweetly Singing*; *Come, Lord, and Tarry Not*; *I Heard the Voice of Jesus Say* and *Deep Down Beneath the Unresting Surge*.

He also wrote extensively on ecclesiastical matters and religion. From the voluminous dome of his head to the fierce wag of his eyebrow and the free-willed spread of his whiskers, one is left with the impression of chap, who would release his merriment in careful measures. However, numerous family

© JEFF DANIELS

tragedies, including the death of five successive children, must have fuelled his faith in a better life to come. It is safe to surmise that the advice offered in his *Christian Treasury* would have enthused employer rather than employee.

The following passage would serve as an example of that.

"In the name of God advancing, sow they seed at morning light, cheerily the furrows turning, labour on with all they might, look not to the far off future, do the work which nearest lies, sow thou must before thou repast, rest at last is labour's prize, standing still is dangerous ever, toil is meant for Christian now, let there be when evening cometh, honest sweat upon thy brow, and the master shall come smiling when work stops at set of sun, saying as he pays thy wages, 'good and faithful man, well done.'"

It seems that William Masters did look to "the far off future" by becoming a sailor, though he must have drawn some comfort from the bulky book, carrying it with him to what became his Liverpool home. With his brothers and sisters, he signed the inside front cover. The book is now kept in the Liverpool home of Jeff Daniels, a qualified chef. William's brother Henry married Mary Clements and had five daughters, the fourth of whom was Veronica. She married Clyde Daniels, a merchant seaman. One of their five children was Jeff, whose dedicated research into his family has been of immense help in compiling this book. I am hugely grateful to him for allowing me to use it.

But we should return to the main narrative in the form that I told it in the café that day.

"As we know, Ann and William Masters lived in the Scotland Road area," I said. "Their son William's birth was registered in Hopwood Street, but he also spent part of his childhood in nearby Eldon Grove. Conditions for most people were grim. Life expectancy was low. Child mortality was high. Into this misery stepped Silas Hocking, a Methodist minister of high morals with a magnificently long beard.

Although born in Cornwall, he worked in Manchester, Liverpool and Southport, preaching to large congregations. But he was also a prolific writer. By far the most popular of his 50 books was *Her Benny*, the story of a brutally treated brother and sister, who run errands and sell matches in the classic tradition, merely to survive. It was published in 1879 and became the first book to sell more than a million copies in the author's lifetime, though Hocking had sold the copyright for £20.

Like Charles Dickens's novels, Hocking's story was serialised, causing a huge stir in the sentimental Victorian public. It was centred in the streets, alleys and courts off Scotland Road."

Outside our café, the sun was in celebratory mood, warming the bugs in the pavement cracks. Yawning workers scurried to their offices. Ron, Tom and Tony were still listening attentively.

"Here I have a much-quoted passage from *Her Benny*," I continued, reaching in my bag for a copy of the book. "Ah yes, here it is.

"Hocking writes: 'And those who have the occasion to penetrate their dark and filthy recesses are generally thankful when they find themselves safe out again. In the winter those streets and courts are kept comparatively clean by the heavy rains; but in the summer the air fairly reeks with the stench of decayed fish, rotting vegetables, and every other conceivable kind of filth. The children that seem to swarm in this neighbourhood are nearly all of a pale, sallow complexion and of stunted growth. Shoes and stockings and underclothing are luxuries that they never know, and one good meal a day is more than they dare hope for. Cuffs and kicks they reckon upon every day of their lives; and in this they are rarely disappointed.'

"You have to remember that Britain then had the greatest empire in the world," I continued. "You could see that in the sailors of many nations, whose ships delivered cargoes to Liverpool, much of which remained desperately poor.

"As Britain established colonies in Africa, there was a feeling that Queen Victoria was the great mother. The natives in those faraway lands were her grateful children. Although such sentiments would be abhorrent today, then even Christians of liberal persuasion regarded the white race as superior. It was our duty to impose our standards on others, irrespective of whether they had developed their own civilizations and systems of religious devotion.

"Perhaps there were moments when William Masters senior wondered if he had been right to leave Jamaica. Anyway, this was the city of the young William. His mother died from cancer when he was young and his father was killed in a steamship accident.

"William and his brothers, James and Henry, were brought up by one of Ann's sisters Mary and her husband Albert. It seems to have been a musical family of some education. William learned to read and write, as well as to play instruments, but he also joined the urchins of the street – a vast cast, who danced and sung, sold trinkets, delivered messages for the toffs, shined shoes, and, more sinisterly looked sweet for those of peculiar tastes and desires. Some strummed banjos; others sang songs or recited poems. Bare-footed artists chalked pictures on the pavements, some beautiful and yearning, to be rubbed away by the rain and the careless feet of the rich. The ladies and gentlemen of the 'quality' chinked their coins on the pavements and opened their face fans. It was a hazardous living and, wheezing in the shadows, the young beggars drifted from pitch to pitch in constant fear of being beaten or arrested – a sure entry to the workhouse on Brownlow Hill.

"William spent his time between street entertainment and selling newspapers. It seems that his performances were recognised as being superior to those of his rivals and he was hired into a formal troupe called Five Boys and appeared in regular venues.

"One day he was sitting in the wings at the Haymarket theatre and was recognised by another artiste performing on stage. William was invited to sing a song. He chose the mildly suggestive *Honeysuckle and the Bee*. The audience loved it, a little black boy singing of love and attraction.

"William Jackson, a prominent impresario, heard news of William's promise and drafted him into his act, called the *Lancashire Lads*, which also featured Charlie Chaplin (1889–1977, a Londoner, whose mixture of clowning and pathos would make him the world's most popular star of silent films).

"In addition to their clog-dancing and singing, William, Charlie and the others played the bones (which would later be replaced by spoons).

"Young Masters toured Britain at least once with the troupe. Soon after that he joined the Jamaican Choir (sometimes called the National Choir of Jamaica, though most of the men and women had been born in Britain). They also appeared in the theatres and music halls, where white singers still blacked their faces with burnt charcoal to perform what was known as 'Negro minstrelsy'.

"In 1908, the Jamaican Choir performed at the Colonial Exhibition staged at Liverpool's St George's Hall.

"With success, William adopted the stage name of Gordon Stretton and played the music halls and jazz clubs such as the Rector's of Paris and London and the Grafton Galleries, London. By then he had his own troupe of dancers and they all appeared in a West End production of *Chu Chin Chow*.

"Drumming was becoming Stretton's forte as a jazzman, but he was also composing songs and tunes. He drummed in the acclaimed William 'Billy' Dorsey band from the US when it toured Britain with its shows, the *Dusky Revels* and *Dark Town Jingles* (composed by Stretton). There really was no escaping the fact that you were an entertainer but also a 'black' entertainer.

"However in 1915 Stretton joined the Army to fight for his country in the Great War. He was badly wounded at Amiens and in the hospital there met Molly Smith, an Irish nurse. They fell in love and married. Stretton's brother James was killed on the Somme. Henry was badly wounded and was invalided out of the Army.

"The young soldiers from Britain, and later America, noted that race prejudice was much less in evidence in some parts of France, which, like Britain, had an extensive African Empire.

"Paris, in particular, seemed to be a city of free and easy ways, where people of different races, creeds and ideas were tolerated, even welcomed. So Stretton moved to Paris in the Jazz Age, when the rich young men and women of America and Europe went crazy after the slaughter of the Great War. It was a time for giddy-talk, flappers, short skirts, drink, drink and more drink, – all this was beautifully chronicled in the novels and short stories of the great American novelist, F. Scott Fitzgerald (1896–1940).

"In Paris, Stretton thrived. By then he was mixing with high society and counted among his friend the Prince of Wales, who would briefly be Edward VIII, before his unyielding desire to marry the American divorcee, Wallis Simpson, led to the abdication of 1936. At their meetings in Paris and London, Stretton called Edward by his first name of 'David' and David called Gordon 'Bill', as he had been to his family and friends on Scotland Road."

From time to time in this narrative, I had to shuffle in my bag for notes, causing my friends some exasperation. But I quickly regained their attention.

"Stretton was also befriended by the great actress, singer and exotic dancer, Josephine Baker (1906–1975). As the victim of prejudice in her native USA, she had adopted French citizenship.

"At the time of their meeting, she was starring in *La Revue Negre*. He performed with her in shows, which he also helped to choreograph. Stretton was starring shows all over France. He crossed the Atlantic regularly and in 1931 his Syncopated Jazz Band recorded the *Satanic Blues* and *Lucky Dog Blues* in New York.

"Eight years earlier, Stretton's Syncopated Six had recorded seven tunes for Pathé, including *Tu Verras Montmartre* (You Will See Montmartre) and *Lovin' Sam*.

"In his 2005 book, *Some Hustling This! Taking Jazz to the World* (1914–1929),

Mark Miller wrote that those two songs were both 'curios among early jazz recordings, if only for Stretton's vaguely operatic manner of singing; he had studied voice in Paris with one of Enrico Caruso's teachers ... Montmartre, a march of sorts, and Lovin' Sam, more conventionally a pop song, receive rousing performances characterized by the fervency of Stretton's vocals and the congested support of his musicians'.

"It was generally agreed that Stretton and his boys put on a lively show and one member of the band attracted attention by dancing and playing the oboe at the same time.

"In the 1920s, Stretton, who had learned to speak French and Spanish and smatterings of other tongues, settled in Argentina, home of the tango, the style of dance music that he loved most.

"He was to become a revered figure in Buenos Aires, travelling to shows in chauffeur-driven limousines. He continued performing until shortly before his death in 1982. Inevitably people will ask why Stretton is not bigger in his native Liverpool – the obvious implication being that there was prejudice against his colour.

There seems to have been some truth in that suggestion. Black performers, even the Jamaican Choir, were seen as something of a novelty and not judged solely on their musical ability.

"They would be expected to include at least some of the American minstrel songs of the white composer Stephen Foster (1826–64) in their repertoire. These included such favourites as *Old Folks At Home*, *Camptown Races*, *Beautiful Dreamer* and *Jeannie with the Light Brown Hair*. There was also some prejudice in London and, to a lesser extent, Paris, where, despite the more worldly mood, emphasis was still placed on colour."

This led to a brief discussion about race relations in Liverpool, where the legacy of slavery is still a dominant theme

My own feeling is that the styles of music favoured by Stretton did not have very widespread appeal, or were little known, in Liverpool, so he took his music to Paris and London and the other great cities of Europe and Latin America. But he is still a Great Liverpudlian.

And I detect a Liverpudlian's understanding of life in the words of one of his hundreds of songs, *The Dancers are Leaving the Ball*.

"At the ball where they danced to the strains of a waltz, there is laughter with tears close behind, there are hearts fit to break though the words are false, there are smiles that just act as a blind, there is age that is his by the powder and paint, there are silks that much poverty cloaks, there are sights that are sad, there are sights that are quaint, there is pain that oft goes with the jokes, many a smile hides a poor breaking heart when the dancers are leaving the ball, when the dancers are leaving the ball."

"Of course, said Ron, "such a successful life might not have been possible if it hadn't been for Kitty Wilkinson."

Stained glass image of Kitty Wilkinson at Liverpool Cathedral

We all nodded, sagely. She was certain to appear in our story before long.

Kitty Wilkinson is one of the most celebrated figures in Liverpool history and the subject of a biography by the local historian Michael Kelly. Her admirers called her the "Saint of the Slums", and "Angel to the Sick".

More importantly, she was a woman who understood that cleanliness prevented the spread of disease. There can be no doubt that thousands more wretched people in Liverpool would have died without her good example. If that sentiment did not apply exactly to the self-reliant and proud Masters' family, it was certainly broadly true. This woman, Kitty, knew that cleanliness was next to godliness.

She was born Catherine Seaward to a thrifty family in Londonderry. Although they were poor, the Seawards were hard working, God-fearing and comparatively well educated.

In common with many Irish people of their generation, they believed that life would be better in England. So, in February 1794, they set sail for Liverpool in a passenger sailing ship. It was bright and sunny when they left Ireland, but the sky darkened dramatically as the approached the English coast. In the ensuing storm, near Hoyle Bank in Liverpool Bay, their ferry was battered by ferocious gales. Mr Seaward was flung overboard and never seen again, but his wife and their two daughters managed to climb into a lifeboat. Then in an act of nature's treachery, Catherine's baby sister was blown from her mother's grip.

The experience had a grievous effect on the emotional stability of the mother and it seems that the little girl, known in Liverpool as Kitty, had to take the initiative if they were to survive.

They found accommodation in Denison Street in the north end of Liverpool. Kitty and her mother worked as domestics in a big and prosperous house, where Mrs Seaward helped the other servants spin and make lace, skills that she had brought with her from Ireland.

At the age of 12, Kitty went to work in a cotton mill in Caton, Lancashire. There, young Tom Wilkinson, a genial fellow of generous ways, heard her sing songs of Liverpool and Ireland in a sweet and clear voice. He was smitten, but there would be a long wait before Kitty became his wife and, to use a more modern expression, his soul mate.

She worked in the mill for seven years, furthering her education at night school, and then returned to Denison Street. By then Mrs Seaward was blind and mentally troubled. But Kitty was an extraordinarily kind woman, who had no qualms about looking after her mother.

At about this time, she married the sailor, Emanuel Demonte, with whom she had two children. But he was drowned at sea three years after their marriage. Despite her own considerable misfortunes, Kitty opened the doors of their home to anyone in need. She also took in washing, which she put through a mangle that had been given to her by a woman of means.

Meanwhile, Tom Wilkinson had taken up employment as a porter in Liverpool. They married and began working together in the washroom in the cellar of their house in Denison Street.

Kitty had no formal medical education, but she did have common sense and an instinctive belief that more stringent standards of hygiene would check the advance of the diseases, often collectively known as "plague".

The prevalent wisdom was that plague lurked in the foul, stinking air, or "miasma", of the cramped courtyards, where sanitation was almost unknown and gin comforted the forlorn mothers. But Kitty thought that disease was carried on filthy linen and clothing.

More and more local people began to accept the sense of her words. In 1832, there was a major outbreak of cholera in Liverpool. This was an opportunity to put her theory to the test.

The women of the neighbourhood carried their bundles of washing to the boiler in Kitty's scullery. In one week alone she washed, dried and returned 34 bedspreads, 158 sheets, 110 blankets, 60 quilts and thousands of items of clothing.

Kitty gathered around her a team of volunteers and, in this atmosphere of cleanliness, not one of them was infected. Slowly the cholera was beaten, but it would return nine more times to Liverpool before 1840. Kitty continued taking in orphans and children in need and she would read them Bible stories and teach them hymns.

However, the authorities were taking notice of her methods and in 1842, with the support of Liverpool Corporation, Kitty and Tom Wilkinson opened Britain's first public baths and wash-house in Upper Frederick Street.

Tom died in 1848, but Kitty lived for another 12 years taking her to what was then the grand old age of 73.

Even Kitty's Christian love and pioneering ideas could do little to help the wretched of her native Ireland, who came to Liverpool in vast numbers during the Potato Famine.

In 1847 alone, 116,000 Irish refugees arrived at the Clarence steamship dock. Many were carrying the seeds of typhus in their bodies. During the year, 60,000 of them were treated for that disease and another 40,000 for dysentery and diarrhoea.

It is now impossible to apply an exact death count. However, in that year of famine and plague, 2,303 people were buried in the grounds and crypt at St Anthony's on Scotland Road, which became the church of the famine. A further 7, 219 paupers were tipped into mass graves at St Mary's churchyard on Cambridge Street. When it was full, more bodies were taken for mass burial to St Martin-in-the-Field on Oxford Road, off Vauxhall Road.

In the slums, priests rested on their haunches to rub their holy oil on the eyelids, the ears, the mouths and the foreheads of those awaiting God. The lice, which spread the disease, crawled into the clothing of the priests. Ten of them died and they were called the Martyrs of the Famine. Some popular historians have romanticised the suffering of that time by calling the Potato Famine the "Great Hunger", but the old description seems more fitting to me.

We cannot know how many lives Kitty saved or extended, but the number would run into thousands. As I wrote before, she had no formal training, but her contribution to nursing was at least equal to that of Florence Nightingale, who would rise to prominence as the Lady with the Lamp during the Crimean War (1854–56). Kitty was carrying a lamp for humanity before that.

Her life is celebrated in a stained glass window at Liverpool Cathedral.

In 1832, when Kitty was battling the cholera raging through the poor part of the port, another Great Liverpudlian, William Ewart Gladstone was returned as the Conservative member for Newark.

Later in his career he would switch to the Liberal Party, serving three times as prime minister (1868–74, 1880–85 and 1892–94). His understanding of life was based on very different experiences to those of Kitty and her friends.

William was born in a three-storey house on Rodney Street, Liverpool. He was the fourth son of Sir John Gladstone and the second son born to his second wife, Anne Mackenzie Robertson, the daughter of Scottish solicitor and aristocrat, Andrew Robertson.

Sir John's first wife, Jane Hall, whom he had married in 1793, died in 1796. In addition to his fine house on Rodney Street, William's father, a merchant, shipbuilder and slave-owner with sugar plantations in Demerara, had also acquired 100 acres of Litherland marsh five miles away on a stretch of coast between Bootle and Waterloo.

Crest of the Right Hon. W. E. Gladstone.

Engraved by Holl (by Permission) from a Photograph by Mayall.

THE RT HON. WILLIAM EWART GLADSTONE. M.P.

He built a grand countryseat there, calling it Seaforth House, after Lord Seaforth, head of his wife's family. The Gladstone family of four sons, two daughters and many servants moved there in 1813. Soon other fashionable families followed and their cluster of houses became Seaforth village.

In 1818, John Gladstone was elected Tory MP for Lancaster and his home soon became a hub for people of distinction, wealth and learning. He invited William Rawson of Cheshire to become vicar of the local church of St Thomas and to start a small boarding school for the Gladstone boys and other sons of privilege. It would prepare them for the great public schools, to which they would be dispatched.

Even in those days, William wrote regular letters to his father, commenting on the seals, which then frequented the shore. On Thursday, March 29, 1821, shortly before he began at Eton, the boy wrote: "The weather has lately been rainy ... The wind was so strong one night that it carried away the wooden roof of one of Mr Rawson's out houses in which he kept his tools. The orchard wall is actually falling inwards. I hope you continue to give my seals your powerful patronage. I am, my dearest father, ever your most affectionate and dutiful son."

This boy would later weather different storms in a life of triumphs and disappointments as one of the great statesmen in British history. He had to make the best of the easy days.

In an earlier letter to his father, he wrote: "I am really writing for very little use and there is a great scarcity of news in this part of the country. The poplars are not all come out into leaf, indeed very few of them, but all the other trees are out and Thomas (probably the gardener) is to begin gravelling."

But from country let us return to town.

Liverpudlians are sentimental. Stories of sorrow and ruin and bravery were made for us.

When I was young and drinking copious quantities of the local cocktail of a brown and bitter (half a pint of bitter in a pint pot finished off with a bottle of brown ale, shaken and stirred), I noticed how popular country and western songs were on the pub jukeboxes.

These were often mawkish offerings about dying dogs, blind orphans, broken love, lonely graveyards and roses. At some point in the night the alcohol and the mood would meet in the squeezing of hands and the clouding of eyes.

In a sense, Silas Hocking's *Her Benny* is a country and western song without the melody, but, as a devout Christian, he dressed his story with the spirit of redemption.

That was missing from the true story of James William Carling, whose life began in similar circumstances to that of William Masters, but ended very differently.

James was the sixth son born to Henry, a maker of boot-blacking, and his wife Rose. They lived in cramped accommodation on Addison Street, off Scotland Road, the area, which had become home to the numerous Irish families, which settled in Liverpool after the Potato Famine.

Worn by the bearing of children, hunger, and the many infections, which had taken root in the filthy courtyards, Rose died.

Henry needed a woman to raise his boys and the nights were long and cold without his Rose. So he married one of the widows in this parish of Holy Cross. The Carling boys were talented and tough. In common with most of the other street kids they could dance, whistle, sing, box – whatever was needed to earn a living as a beggar.

But James and his older brother, Henry, had a precocious gift for drawing, when they could afford the chalk and paints. Their stepmother was not slow to realise the potential of her new brood. Should they not go out to earn their living and put some food on the table?

This is what little, sad-eyed James had to say about his stepmother and, in the words chosen, you can hear the sarcasm and bitterness that is still a strong part of Liverpudlian speech, though the vocabulary used then was richer than you would expect these days.

"Starved by a stepmother of a very unusual disposition, I sallied out into the world like Jack of the fairy tales to seek my fortune, and a living as well, at the grand old age of five."

James, with his brothers, Willy, Johnny and Henry, became a beggar, earning coins by drawing pictures on the pavements.

Well, I think about life and its strange twists. We all do. But is there anything sadder than an artist creating beauty in stone, only to see his work lost forever in the pattering of rain and the careless rub of shoe leather?

We know from later work that James, or "Little Chalky", was a good artist. And it seems that all the boys were educated and familiar with the works of Shakespeare and the great poets, though their ability to acquire such learning amid such hardship must fire our admiration.

They performed outside the theatres – reciting, drawing and singing, sometimes even earning enough to pay for their admission. These opportunities, of course, would have furthered their knowledge of drama, as well as popular entertainments.

The family probably brought their love of literature with them from Ireland, where poverty and illiteracy did not always run together.

The boys were naturally sensitive and cultured. Teachers at Holy Cross School, which they attended when they were not on the streets earning the

James William Carling in a
begging pose

© JAMES WILLIAM CARLING GALLERY, MAGGIE
MAY'S CAFÉ, LIVERPOOL

money to support their stepmother, might have advanced these qualities. We don't really know but it is remarkable that a love of learning should have thrived in such wretched circumstances.

However, it is also evident from the journals written by the brothers in later life that they were "hard" and quick with their fists. This enabled them to protect their pitches from the advances of other beggars. Additionally, they had to defend themselves against the Peelers (policemen), who would often lash-out with staves when moving them on. That certainly happened on Bold Street, the fashionable parade of Liverpool's rich shoppers – the family's of the port's emerging merchant princes, whose money still shone rather too brightly, having not had the time to mature into good manners and dignity.

James Carling had good manners and dignity. They had been given to him by God and he nurtured them both, seeing the world through the eyes of a child, but with great clarity, sharpened by the pain of bruises delivered by those policemen on behalf of the toffs.

"Bold Street! My heart sickens at your name," he wrote. "And well it might, for not only could I not draw in that street, I could not walk on it. The sight of a ragged coat was enough to bring the harsh 'move on', or, what was worse, the most brutal application of the staff. On Bold Street, promenade of the local aristocracy, the gocking (pavement artist) did not draw."

This is a Liverpool story, so it is perhaps not entirely surprising that the change in James's fortunes came on Christmas Eve, 1865, after he was arrested on Lime Street for begging.

To use one of Ron Formby's favourite expressions, "You couldn't make that up." Indeed not.

The wraith-like boy was flung into a cell at Cheapside police station, where he stayed for a week before being transferred to St George's Industrial School run by Father James Nugent, who also fits perfectly into this story.

Father (later Monsignor) Nugent was one of nine children born into a Liverpool family. He was a man of learning and piety remembered particularly for his work with the destitute.

A year after his death a statue to his memory was erected in St John's Gardens behind St George's Hall. At this stage we are stepping among the saints. Nugent and his staff spotted James' potential and after six years the boy left the school as a man of learning, his natural talent as an artist having also been given the opportunity to flourish.

By then Henry Carling, who had moved to Philadelphia, had improved greatly as a portraitist. He paid the fare for James to join them in the USA. The atmosphere there was more congenial.

Stories about the brothers appeared in the local Press and they were billed as the "lightning caricaturists", specialising in instant drawings of prizefighters, entertainers and US presidents. They became celebrities themselves.

It might have been in these more prosperous times that James developed his liking for drink.

The brothers had come a long way from the fetid slums and sullen skies of Liverpool. They were appearing at circuses and travelling shows and their suits were tailored from fine cloth. Strangers would wave to them on the sidewalks.

Henry was also winning commissions to do portraits of the wives and daughters of successful men. There was less class prejudice in the USA. The country was not yet 100 years old and out on the prairies and deserts, the Sioux, the Cheyenne, the Apache and their fierce brothers were giving the American cavalry a torrid time.

To cap their good fortune and perhaps to match Henry's standing in more serious circles, James decided on a scheme that could have secured his reputation for posterity. But before raising your hopes, you mustn't forget that this story began in a city where triumph and tragedy rub noses.

In 1883, the fashionable *Harper's* magazine had started a competition to illustrate a new edition of Edgar Allan Poe's poem, *The Raven*, first published in 1845. This was James's moment. If successful his name would be forever associated with that of Poe (1809–49), one of the great names in American literature. He worked night and day at his home in Chicago, tormented by the images that rapped and tapped in his fevered mind. In the end he produced 33 paintings, but against him was Gustave Dore (1832–83), the celebrated French painter, who had already illustrated editions of the Bible and Dante's *Inferno*, as well as Dante's *Purgatorio* and *Paradiso*.

It was a bitter blow for James, who returned to England four years later.

We are not entirely certain about why he made this fateful decision. He seemed to want to collect some songs and ballads left by his grandfather, which would suggest that singing was another of his extraordinary gifts. He was also hoping to study at the National School of Art in London.

Whatever the reason, he returned to Liverpool in poor health and without any obvious means of support. On June 17, 1887, he was admitted to the workhouse on Brownlow Hill. On July 9, he died, probably from consumption, the coughing disease that left its victims pale and owl-eyed.

This man had winced to the beat of police staves and seen his work vanish beneath the feet of the rich, but he had also heard applause and tasted a little of the high life in a distant land.

Little Chalky's emaciated body was carried to Walton Park Cemetery, where it was buried in an unmarked mass grave with those of 15 other paupers. But in 1984, with interested in Carling's work growing, a marker was put on the spot.

Back in America Henry had exhibited his brother's Raven paintings in 1930. Six years later, his daughter, Marion, donated them to the Edgar Allan

Poe Museum in Richmond, Virginia, where they are now kept in special conditions to prevent them deteriorating.

Ron Formby and the historian Michael Kelly campaigned vigorously to ensure that James William Carling's name should be known by 2008, Liverpool's years as the European Capital of Culture.

In 2007, their ambitions were realised when John Lea, proprietor of Maggie May's café on Bold Street, allowed the upstairs room to be converted into a gallery dedicated to the memory of James William Carling. Prints of his own work were displayed alongside the work of today's Liverpool artists. An annual pavement artists' competition was started in 2008 and named in his honour.

Carling's triumphant return to Bold Street may have been greeted by a weary smile somewhere in the sky – who knows?

The story of James William Carling is very dear to Ron.

At last we had finished our tea and scones in the café on Old Hall Street and, in the style of tourists, we wandered across the lovely gardens of Liverpool Parish Church (Our Lady and St Nicholas), popularly called the Sailors' Church.

People have been worshipping on these salted grounds for more than 800 years.

A few hundred yards down the dock road, on the Pier Head, is the Royal Liver Building, on which perch the two famous Liver Birds, totems of the port, seen on Liverpool Football Club shirts, civic documents, publications and postcards, as well as in many hundreds of public and private buildings.

In fact, new Liver Birds are hatching all the time, as people seek to capitalise on what is one of the world's most potent symbols, immediately identified with Liverpool. They stand comparison to New York's Statue of Liberty, or Liberty Enlightening the World, the 150ft colossus by the sculptor August Bartholdi, which was placed on an iron framework designed by Gustave Eiffel, who also gave Paris its 984ft tower.

By far the most famous of these birds are the pair on the Liver Building – one looking to sea and the other inland, poses that have made it impossible for them to breed.

Indeed, it is not known whether we have two males, two females, or one of each gender. But we do know that each one is 18ft tall with a wingspan of 24ft. All Liverpudlians know the legend. If they should fly away, the city would cease to be. But we can rest easy. Squadrons of pigs will take to the air before those immobile birds.

All the Liver Birds in Liverpool can trace their ancestry back the reign of King John, whose Royal Charter in 1207 enabled Liverpool to develop into a major port. It was decided then that Liverpool should have a corporate seal with the heraldic eagle, which the king had adopted from St John the Evangelist.

In creating the seal, the local artists had been influenced by the cormorant, then a common wader in the river. This could explain the seaweed or laver hanging from the bird's beak, instead of the sprig of broom favoured by St John's eagle. The result of all this was a proliferation of Liver Birds in the city.

Of course, you'd expect the name of the artist responsible for the famous birds on Liver Building to be widely known. But you would be wrong.

In 1908, work had begun on the Royal Liver Building, designed by the architect Walter Aubrey Thomas. An international competition was held to choose a design for the two birds, which were to sit atop the clock towers.

Details of this competition were read by Carl Bernard Bartels, the son of Carl Julius Bartels, a wood carver from Germany's Black Forest region.

The father taught the son his craft at their studio in Stuttgart. In 1887, the son came to Britain. By then he was married to Mathilde Zappe.

The couple liked England, adopting British nationality and settling in the London Borough of Haringey, where they had a son, Bernard Charles Bartels, and a daughter, Maggie.

The father was establishing himself as a fine carver and artist and his drawings of the birds won the competition for the building, which was being constructed for the Royal Liver Friendly Society.

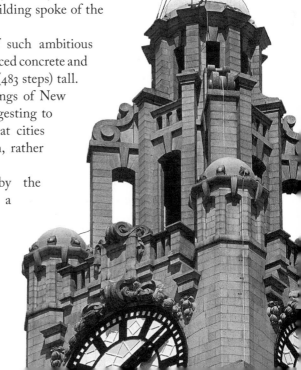

It had been formed as a burial society in 1850 by a group of men who met in the Lyver Inn, St Anne Street, Liverpool. Their original concern was to help people meet the growing costs of a decent burial and funeral. However, it quickly widened its embrace and in 1857 changed its name to the Royal Liver Friendly Society and later to Royal Liver Assurance. The building spoke of the city's confidence.

It was the first in Britain of such ambitious dimensions to be built from reinforced concrete and is 310ft long, 177ft wide and 167ft (483 steps) tall. Its similarity to the grand buildings of New York is immediately obvious, suggesting to the romantic that these two great cities are joined by the Atlantic Ocean, rather than separated by it.

Bartels' birds were made by the Bromsgrove Guild (1899–1960), a group of talented young artists and craftsmen, also responsible for the chancel gates and the reredos at Liverpool Cathedral.

The Royal Liver Building was opened to considerable fanfare and some criticism (inevitably about its modernity) in 1911.

Three years later the Great War broke out. Anti-German sentiments swelled in Liverpool and other towns and cities.

In such times, memories are short. Pork butchers from the Hohenlohe area of German had been knotting their sausages in Liverpool since the middle of the nineteenth century. The fruity smells of baking and the steam from the sauerkraut joined the air of a city already in riches in aromas. At the time lobscouse, a Norwegian stew, was favoured by Liverpool sailors, leading to Scousers, the common name for Liverpudlians – sometimes used with respect and sometimes not.

"Krauts" as a derogatory name for Germans was not widely used until the Second World War. Many older Liverpudlians, or Liverpolitans, if you want to be stately about it, will remember "Whacker" being a more widely used name for a citizen of Liverpool – deriving from the use of "wack" or "whacker" as an affectionate term of address on the pavement, as in "arrright whack".

But by the mid sixties, it was being replaced by Scouse, which also referred to the stew and the Liverpool accent.

In times of war, though, expressions of endearment or gentle mockery count for nothing. Old friends crossed to the other side when they saw someone with a German name approaching. Germans had worked in Liverpool factories, particularly the Tate & Lyle sugar refinery, as well as the butchers' shops. But the authorities rounded them up.

Bartels was sent to the Knockaloe Camp on the Isle of Man, though his family had been naturalised Britons for more than 20 years. Conditions were harsh but camaraderie developed, particularly among his fellow artists.

Anti-German feelings in Liverpool reached their zenith in 1915 when a German U-boat sank the *Lusitania* off the coast of Ireland. She had been on her way to the port from New York. Riots broke out and German shops and properties were looted. During this time of upheaval and sorrow carried on a strong patriotic mood, Bartels' blueprints and designs for the Liver Birds were mysteriously mislaid.

After the war, he returned to Germany for a while, leaving family in London, but they were quickly reunited. Bartels continued as a carver. His work in Durham Cathedral and some stately homes, as well as the Liver Birds, tell of his contributions to British life.

In the Second World War, he worked on artificial limbs for those who had been maimed in the fighting. He died in London in 1955.

His significant part in Liverpool's history would have remained largely forgotten, if it had not been for Tim Olden, his grandson and a graphic artist from Southampton. He campaigned to have Bartels' memory restored in Liverpool for 2007, the 800th anniversary of it being granted King John's Charter, and 2008, its year as the European Capital of culture.

The Friends of Liverpool Monuments and the Merseyside Civic Society enthusiastically supported him, helping Bartels receive some belated recognition for his great part in the story of Liverpool's famous, flightless birds.

Liverpool is an international city, but it is also a village. A visitor can walk from Lime Street railway station to the Pier head in about 20 minutes. The cathedrals, the Cavern Club, the shops and most of the inner city sites, including the extended Leeds and Liverpool Canal, are all within easy walking distance. If you are reasonably well known in the city, you are constantly bumping into people you know.

Friends cluster on the pavements outside the pubs and the cafés for a chat.

And sitting on a bench at the old Pier Head was Kay Kelly, another Liverpool patriot, who, like Ron Formby, had devoted much of her life to sticking up for the underdog and those oppressed by authority.

Pale with a green-eyed stare, Kay possessed tremendous inner-strength, which had been reinforced by her absolute devotion to the Holy Virgin, Mary Mother of Jesus, who had appeared to her in times of trouble and illness.

Well, that's what Kay said and she said it with a conviction that could crumble granite. But she was not always so certain about everything.

"Am I a pain in the butt?" she asked me one day, having spent most of that morning liquefying some hapless wretch from officialdom, who was only doing his job when he cut off a family's electricity or raised the rent or cancelled the pensioners' Christmas party. She might have been slight of frame, but she could advance over the hill like a rumbling panzer division to the desk of a petty bureaucrat.

"No, no, you're not a pain in the butt. You're a saint," I said, curling my toes and gazing deep into the sky for a sign.

"Ah well, she's a good Catholic girl," people would have said a generation or two ago, when the size of a person's soul was measured by their genuflections.

And there had been occasions when Kay and her soul were a tight fit in the church doorway.

"God love him/her," she said herself, in celebration of human weakness, after hearing of some escapade involving one of her friends. You might have suffered a terrible fall but you'll still find divine grace.

Kay rose to prominence in the 1970s when she was suffering from Hodgkin's disease and began a fund to raise money for cancer research at Clatterbridge Hospital, Wirral.

At one point it seemed likely that she would die then and her frail body was carried into St Mary of the Angels Church on Everton Brow. Some years later she told me what had happened that day.

Queen Victoria riding at St George's Hall
© PETER KENNERLEY

"I had said to the doctors, 'Thine will be done'. You know, you give yourself to God and he can give you back. That's the way I have worked ever since and I am still here. Anyway, I was sitting at the back and behind the altar is a massive picture of Our Blessed Lady.

"She looked down and I looked up and she said, 'Don't worry everything is going to be all right'. There were times when I was so ill that I thought I was hearing things, but there was this voice within me telling me I would be all right."

Faith of that sort is not fashionable these days. People shrink from such revelations. And yet, and yet, you know, deep within us all there is a yearning. Most of us suppress it, but it was Kay's reason for being.

That is not to say that she wa a religious bore, far from it. Her conversation sparkled, but she lamented the lack of faith and truth in many of the church leaders, who have hopped from promotion to promotion, in much the same way as company executives.

Her appeal raised £1m for cancer research. She also helped raise the money to send people to Lourdes. The proceeds from the 10,000 sales of her book, *With Love from Kay*, were donated to Mother Teresa's charity. She met Pope Paul II in the Vatican in 1979.

Kay's greatest devotion was to St Mary of the Angels Church, where she felt the love of the Blessed Virgin. The church had been built with money from Amy Elizabeth Rosalie Imrie (1870–1944), the adopted daughter of William and Hannah Imrie.

William Imrie (1836–1906) was a man of immense wealth and charity. In 1870 he began the White Star shipping line with his friend and former colleague Thomas Ismay.

Imrie was less demonstrative than his partner and he was possessed of a steady and determined temperament, helping guide the shipping line from the days of sail into the mechanical world. He died before the line's most publicised ship, the *Titanic*, sank in 1912. From him and her quietly devoted mother, Amy cultivated a strong religious faith, which would lead to her entering holy orders and becoming a nun with the Poor Clares.

Between 1907 and 1910, she gave a considerable part of the family fortune to building the church, which she dedicated to the people of Liverpool in perpetuity. She filled it with ecclesiastical treasures from Italy, so that our poor would have a sense of Rome's wonders.

Amy, who was appointed the Mother Superior at a convent in Cornwall, also arranged for the family's grand home in Mossley Hill, Liverpool, to be converted into a convent.

In 2001, following an examination of the viability of "inner-city parishes", the Roman Catholic authorities closed St Mary of the Angels Church. Kay immediately began a campaign to have it retained as a place of worship.

English Heritage recognised its importance as a building by granting it Grade II-listed status. This meant that it couldn't be demolished without public inquiry. More recently, the Royal Liverpool Philharmonic Orchestra has been using the building for rehearsals.

Kay held the values of old Liverpool. "The River Mersey runs in my veins," she told me. "I don't depend on anyone for a living. I don't have to say, 'Yes sir, no sir, three bags full sir'. It is the people out there I am fighting for." Kay died earlier this year.

Ah yes, "the people", all the Great Liverpudlians, that's what it is all about. So we have the artists, Tony Brown and Tom Murphy, whose work helps make this a city of immortality, and then you have the people themselves – men and women, like Kay Kelly and Ron Formby, whose spirit crosses the generations, always reaching for the future, but never forgetting the past.

And through their eyes pass the smiling ghosts of Kitty Wilkinson; Little Chalky; Gordon Stretton, the black boy among the ragamuffins; and a lad called Gladstone, who saw the seals play in a mighty river.

5

WOMEN OF PASSION

"You know, they have more passion than a pavilion full of rugby players preparing for a big match," said the fellow in a woollen cap of the sort favoured by bookies on race courses, as he squeezed through the back door of the cab in his broad overcoat, made in the days when a good tailor knew his Donegal tweed.

"More passion than a pavilion full of rugby players?" I said with a hint of incredulity in my tone. "Surely, they have more passion than a cathedral full of priests."

For I knew that my good friend Michael Kelly was speaking of women - Liverpool women in particular, as he stepped into the cab on that bitter night before the Christmas of 2009, the start of the first real winter we'd had for years. It was a bit like the old days that we both remembered so well – of burst pipes and permanent threats of snow from the brooding sky, when you could scratch your names in the ice on the inside of the window.

But on this night, freezing fog was falling across the land, over the hard, rutted fields. We had both been on speaking engagements in West Lancashire and had agreed to share a taxi home. As part of his job as a local historian, Michael addresses small groups in those scout huts and community halls, where the speaker's voice has to compete with the coughs and wheezes of the temperamental radiator, which seems to have been there, contentedly leaking, since before the beginning of time. It is part of the charm of the old country. I am also an occasional public speaker and try to amuse similar groups of women with stories from my life in journalism. In my experience, however, the rumbling radiator always wins – unless the caretaker is still in the house with his trusty spanner to silence the infernal contraption.

The Queen Victoria Monument near James Street railway station

But Michael, a fine tenor, can make his voice soar through any building. He is also an expert on woman – not in the popular sense, as practised by those magazine Romeos, but in the deeper way of understanding their often unsung contributions to the city, which at first glimpse appears to be dominated by men. Certainly, most of the paintings and sculptures feature men, though there is a fair scattering of angels winging about the scene.

Anyway, a couple of years back, Michael embarked on his great project of writing a book about the women of Liverpool, I had suggested the title, Mothers of the City, which he had liked. In return he had invited me to write his foreword, which I was honoured to do.

We both knew then that it would be a difficult task. As we have said, men had been in charge in most of those fields of activity that made Liverpool a great city and one of the most celebrated ports in the world – pop music, football, boxing, industry, seafaring, politics and religion.

"Indeed," said Michael, "but we have in our minds the picture of an iceberg – with the men taking the glory and preening themselves at the top, while the women are the power underneath, the true power."

Michael was thinking of his own grandmothers, Mary Doyle and Mary Kelly, who had played a big part in his upbringing in the Scotland Road area of Liverpool. "It was very difficult for them to feed large families like mine," he said. As he spoke, I was reminded of a certain miracle involving a clutch of fish, a few loaves and a lot of people.

"Yes, it was very difficult," Michael continued. "One of the delicacies, quite a delicacy all over Liverpool on Sunday morning, was salt-fish, which would be bought on the Saturday. It was like a board, which would be left to soak overnight to get the salt out of it. It would be put on the stove in the morning and left for a couple of hours to boil up. It was lovely.

"The first house I can remember had two bedrooms and there was a cold water tap in the pantry. Most families had a tin bath and perhaps three or four people would use the same water. The women were in charge and they led our lives."

"To some extent, the role of women has been a problem in the teaching of all British history," I said. "When I was young women were generally ignored, except for Florence Nightingale and the queens, Boadicea, Elizabeth and Victoria, with everyone being taught to recite the names of the wives of Henry VIII, whose heads were chopped off. Otherwise, we were taught about triumphant men – the kings, explorers, theologians, warriors, inventors and politicians, with much time dedicated to their crushing of weaker people from overseas. Of course, we were taught never to trust the French."

"All that is true and it has made the emergence of successful women all the more remarkable," said Michael. "And we have the names of individual women from Merseyside, whose achievements will never be forgotten, perhaps the most famous of these in the popular imagination are Bessie Braddock and Cilla Black. But I also think of Rose Heilbron, one of the most distinguished lawyers of her generation; Lizzie Christian, the barrow girl, whose face is rooted in the heart of the city; Agnes Jones, the pioneering nurse; Ethel Austin, a wonderful businesswoman; Lottie Dod, the brilliant all-round sportswoman, and Felicia Hemans, the writer, whose most famous poem began, 'The boy stood on the burning deck'."

"I sometimes think of how much more successful Glenda Jackson would have been, if she had stayed in acting instead of going into politics," I said. "She may not agree with this, but good actors are held in higher esteem than good politicians. You have to be a really great politician to be remembered. My natural feel for the underdog also turns me towards Beryl Marsden, thought by many contemporaries to have been the best female singer of the Merseybeat years. She was eclipsed by Cilla in terms of record sales and TV shows and yet she has never quite disappeared."

"Yes, but there is something more than that," said Michael. "I remember women being the backbone of the whole community when I was growing up. They were saints really, able to turn a few spuds into a banquet and, even more importantly, they could restore our spirits on those days when the whole world seemed against us. When the men turned to drink, the women often turned to prayer – or, more practically, just getting on with life, walking down the streets with bundles of washing carried on their heads, like huge turbans. There wasn't much time for self-pity in their lives. They knew they were responsible for the children, bringing on another generation."

"The church was very important to people then," I said. "The parish churches, where boys and girls toddled in for baptism, strode down the aisle on their wedding days, and were carried out in boxes at the end. Priests have told me that it was the women who kept the churches going in the hard times. They were the ones who were so devout, perhaps in some cases seeing themselves as the successors of the Blessed Virgin. At Christmas the mothers come into their own. It's a very poetic time for me. I think of the ghosts being sucked back into their warm skins at Christmas. There is this sense of motherhood being everywhere."

Outside, the cab the fog was deepening. Orange headlamps pierced the gloom, but then that fog swirled and gathered like a wall of ghosts to cut off their beams.

"I can almost hear it now," I said, recalling my own boyhood in a middle-class suburb – in some ways very far from the poor streets and yet only half a mile away by other measurements.

"It's like a poem to me, always in my mind at this time of year. You know, the dark hush, the strange sigh that rises from the ground to veil all the land like a warm yawn shortly before six o'clock on Christmas Eve. Then the mothers at last stretch their tired legs on footstools, just for a moment or two, happy that everything has been done to make tomorrow perfect for everyone.

The shops are shuttered, the exhausted tills have trilled "no more", and loose tea is settling in the old, chapel-brown pot. Of course, there are jobs still to be done – who will stuff that bald bird in the kitchen, whose arms are strong enough to slice the turnip, who will refill the coal scuttle, who will roast the chestnuts, who will dress the tree with the final sprig of tinsel and twist the star of Bethlehem, so that it shines from the lounge window at the sky beyond; and who is going to hide Father Christmas's crimson stocking of jagged parcels, tangerines and pink-tailed sugar mice in the cupboard under the stairs? These things don't happen by magic you know. Someone has to do them. But, just for that moment on Christmas Eve, there is silence, blissful peace; and the dog slumbers and shudders deeply on the rug with one eye open and the other eye dreaming of bones and snouting in the wild old country of red berries and frozen leaves of mystical green, where holy men padded in leather boots. This is the time of women. The past and present are as one, reaching to each other. Then in the distance the gravel crunches and couples link arms, like Victorian pictures, and they walk into the sandstone church. There, the wooden baby waits in the Sunday school cradle. Hark! The Herald Angels Sing. A ship hoots on the river. Snow is falling. Even now I can see my late mother in the kitchen, her hands pink on the powdered table, as she rolls pastry into strips to be cut by the serrated crown into mince pies ready for the oven. But who is that slumped and snoozing in the corner? Who's been at the sherry again? He looks familiar to me."

"And to me," said Michael. "The old romantic has had one too many – a sight I have seen before. But that is a fine picture of motherhood at Christmas. It is their time – the Son of God, born to a mother on Earth.

"But you are right about the women generally, especially the way that they kept the families together. Every shining doorstep and every well-nourished child was a testament to the contribution made by women to this city. The people on the streets understand it. In his song *Let It Be*, Paul McCartney sings, 'When I find myself in times of trouble, Mother Mary comes to me, speaking words of wisdom, let it be …'

"That sums it up for me. The role of women hasn't been given sufficient recognition in the formal history books, but the memory of those women strides on in the faces and in the blood of the young people advancing through the prosperous city and so it will go continue from generation to generation. They are the living monuments to the women who have passed on. Women remain far more active than men in the community – in the charities, the welfare services, the schools, increasingly in politics and, of course, our homes. They are unswervingly loyal to their men and to their city. They are the Mothers of the City. Let's drink to that."

"There is something very Irish about you, Michael," I said, "but, then, there is something very Irish about Liverpool."

6

PAST & PRESENT

In the oil-stained water, where fish no longer swam, the ferry's coughing engines trembled the upper deck, upon which strode the businessmen in their dark suits, swishing brollies and briefcases to the rhythm of their steps.

The wind was keen and the gulls winged to the shore. Behind us the green dome glowed with stately reserve on Birkenhead Town Hall, where the turbaned cleaners dry-mopped the mosaic floor, sucked their cigarettes and gossiped.

Finally, the juddering boat shuddered to a halt against a cushion of tyres hanging down the Liverpool wall of the River Mersey.

Two little boys crept, pale-kneed and big-eyed, along the hooded gangway to the grand buildings at the Pier Head.

This was Liverpool, the Big City, the Pool, the most glamorous place on Earth, and the business men were pushing their way past us, so they would not be late at the desks in the shipping offices, the banks, the shops, the many agencies and insurance offices – all those dens of commerce.

Michael Jones and I were just friends, children, who seemed no bigger than sugar bags, gazing at the grand monuments of a port, which served a great empire.

"Gosh," I said.

"Golly," he said. "Isn't everything huge?"

We gazed in wonder.

You could see Liverpool from both our bedroom windows on the high ground of Birkenhead, but you had to cross the river to see exactly how big the buildings were, as they bruised God's sky.

With that we went to a café, where a Chinaman served us. There we were, David Charters and young Michael Jones, drinking tea, which had been brought by ship all the way from India, to be poured from a silver pot by a waiter from an even more distant land.

We didn't know then that the Chinese community in Liverpool was one of the oldest in Europe, starting in the 1870s when the Blue Funnel line opened its steamship link to China.

Pigtailed Chinese sailors became a familiar sight in the city. Others ran boarding houses, laundries and chop-suey houses, even a private detective agency.

The census of 1881 recorded only 15 Chinese residents in Birkenhead and Liverpool, but there must have been many others living here on a temporary basis.

Anyway, the Chinese waiter poured the tea for Michael Jones, a good name for a Celt, with its hint of biscuit-brown Welsh chapels and Irish malt.

This was my first memory of Liverpool, though I would soon visit the city more regularly, on the train as well as the ferry.

My youngest sister was a sculpture student at the Liverpool School of Art and on occasions she would take me to the cafés, where she met her friends. Those were the beatnik days when pale faced boys and girls, dressed in priestly black, talking of the Bomb's mushroom cloud, as they dunked their biscuits in espresso coffee and read the poems of the American Beats.

Christmas shopping in Liverpool was another treat, starting with lunch in the Kardomah café – before watching from little more than counter-height in

The Liverpool Athenaeum, a place of learning in the city since 1797

© THE ATHENAEUM

Mersey ferry
© PETER KENNERLEY

the department stores, such as Lewis's and the old George Henry Lee's, as the mothers stacked their parcels into wobbly mountains, while shepherding their children towards the grottos, where sat Father Christmas in his magnificent crimson robes – or so they seemed in the eyes of the memory.

And on the crowded platforms of the underground stations, children held hands with their mums and thought about mince pies, white icing, snow, fairy lights and the man himself, ringing his bells on the all-night sleigh-ride.

Then came the tingling morning itself when, in the half-light, you reached for the stocking – bulging and swollen with those high-scented tangerines, dates from exotic lands, and little toys that sprang to life with the twisting of a key.

Liverpool was Christmas to me.

The other man to be seen by young Christmas shopper was the naked chap, who was attached to Lewis's store in 1959. He had been sculpted by Jacob Epstein and was officially called Liverpool Resurgent but we called him Dickie Lewis for reasons that would not have unduly taxed Sherlock Holmes.

"We meet under a statue exceedingly bare," is part of the chorus from the Liverpool folk anthem, *In My Liverpool Home*, written by Peter McGovern (1927–2006). The nakedness of the statue stirred considerable controversy, though McGovern's song demonstrates considerable ecumenical diplomacy in the line, "if you want a cathedral we've got one to spare".

But which one? You make your mind up. In fact, these days many lamp-lit choristers shout "two" when the sentiment reaches their tonsils – a sure sign of changing times.

Now, there are even more shops and tall buildings in Liverpool, partly as a result of developments before and after the city's year as the European Capital of Culture.

People are particularly excited by the Liverpool One shopping centre, built for 160 "famous" high street stores, as well as offices, cafés and restaurants on a 42-acre site. I know people who love it. To them it is the future. Well, I am an old curmudgeon, who preferred things the way they were, so my opinion on this subject counts for little.

But Liverpool has some 40,000 resident college and university students and they have transformed the nightlife. On a summer's evening in 2010, I attended the birthday dinner of a friend at the Liverpool Athenaeum in Church Alley, off Church Street.

This is a grand old place of learning founded in 1797 by those who felt that the brash port needed dignity and scholarship, as well as money and the adventurous spirit.

Down the years it has attracted Liverpool's finest thinkers – the writers, scientists, theologians, lawyers, teachers, philanthropists, philosophers, as well as a few cads, garter-snappers, fast-dealers, jewellers and duellers.

After a splendid meal, my wife and I stepped into the summer's balm to hail a taxi to take us back to Birkenhead.

Hot juices flowed long in the city that night, as the tall black cabs paraded along the road, their back doors winging wide, so that young men and women, dressed as tarts and bishops, nurses and vampires, Robin Hood, Red Indian squaws and cavaliers, cavorted onto the pavements. The low-slung cars crept forward. honking their hooters, the drivers staring helplessly from the windows, as they inched forwards.

Carousing girls clip-clopped down the stone stairs of the pubs in high-heeled chaos.

A lump rose in my throat as I stood there remembering how I had first stared in wonder in another age at the shimmering monuments of this port. This was a city fit for princes, yet still I heard the tinkle of coins in the beggar's saucer.

Sometimes I feel a stranger in this city of storytellers and minstrels, but there are days when I step out and see the fruit stalls with their pyramids of oranges and grapes, the peaches and apples, the pears and exotic nectarines.

The air smells sweet and old and, for those moments, I feel I belong here.

Either way, I know that for me, writing about Liverpool has always been a privilege.

BIOGRAPHICAL INDEX

T HIS INDEX GIVES MORE INFORMATION about many of the people mentioned in the first five chapters of this book. Their names are listed in the order of their appearances in the text.

DAVE HICKSON (1929–). Swashbuckling English centre forward, whose glory years were in the 1950s. He is the only man to have played at a senior level for Everton, Liverpool and Tranmere Rovers. During two spells at Everton, he played in 225 matches, scoring 95 goals. He scored 37 goals for Liverpool in 95 outings and 21 for Tranmere Rovers in 45 appearances.

His blond good looks and bold approach to the game made him a hero to thousands. Despite his popularity, Dave was always a modest man. I interviewed him and his wife, Pat, at their home in 2008.

This is how he described his glory years at Everton. "I was on £20 a week, which wasn't bad at all then. At the time my dad was on £15 a week at Bowater's (a paper mill in Ellesmere Port). That was great. I was getting more than my own dad! But it's unbelievable what they get today. Although I didn't get much from football financially, I did well from football because of the enjoyment. I love it … It's been brilliant."

In common with many modest men, Dave doesn't fully appreciate just how much he meant to his admirers. We will never forget him.

WILLIAM RALPH "DIXIE" DEAN (1907–1980) was probably the greatest English centre forward. Born in Birkenhead, he played 30 times for Tranmere Rovers (1923–1925), scoring 27 goals. He was with Everton between 1925 and 1937, making 399 appearances and scoring 349 goals. He was an England international from 1927 until 1932, scoring 18 goals in his 16 appearances.

His name has been passed down through the generations of Evertonians, as an example of the club's motto turned into flesh and blood – Nil Satis Nisi Optimum (only the best satisfies). Nothing but the best is good enough.

John Keith, broadcaster/journalist and one of Dean's biographers explained his enduring appeal. "When you mention his name there is a resonance of greatness that I don't think is engendered by anyone else," he said.

Tom Murphy's magnificent sculpture of Dixie Dean stands outside Goodison Park, home of Everton.

TOMMY EGLINGTON (1923–2004) was a winger and forward for Everton between 1946 and 1957, scoring 82 goals in 428 outings. Affectionately known as "Ego", he moved to Tranmere Rovers, where he stayed until 1961, making 172 appearances and scoring 36 goals. As an Irish international, he played for both the Republic and Northern Ireland. He gained six caps with the IFA, which then governed football in the North, and 24 for the FAI, which was responsible for the Republic.

HANNIBAL BARCA (247–182 BC): Carthaginian general and one of the greatest military strategists in history. His extraordinary feat of crossing the Alps with his army and elephants from the Carthaginian Empire in Spain to Italy, and then inflicting a series of humiliating defeats on much larger Roman armies, has stirred artists, writers and soldiers. He is, therefore, a figure of romance, synonymous with bravery and a willingness to fight and succeed against the odds, true Liverpudlian qualities.

Carthage in North Africa, near Tunis, was the grand trading port of the ancient world, bringing in spices, jewels, fruits, dyes and other treasures from many lands, including tin from Cornwall. With its rich merchants in their splendid palaces and its massive public buildings, Victorian Liverpool, which handled cargoes from the British Empire and the Americas, was often compared to opulent Carthage.

Lubeck, the Baltic port in northwest Germany, founder of the mediaeval Hanseatic League of trading cities, had also been called "the Carthage of the North" because of its prosperity. However, in 146BC, after three bloody wars, envious Rome destroyed Carthage. Liverpool and Lubeck both go on.

ROY RACE OF THE ROVERS was a fictional footballer, who first appeared in the Tiger comic in 1954. He played on until his career was ended by the loss of a foot in a helicopter accident in 1993, a serious handicap for a footballer in the top flight. But his exploits for Melchester Rovers had come to symbolise the glamour and Corinthian spirit often missing in real football. Young Everton fans once had their own Roy in Dave Hickson. But Bobby Charlton of England and Manchester United came even closer to the ideals of Roy of the Rovers.

HAMON DE MASCI (1129–1216) was the third baron of Dunham Massey (Masci). His family came over with William the Conqueror. He ordered the building of Birkenhead Priory.

ROBERT DE WALEY was thought to have been the first prior at Birkenhead Priory built around 1150, the oldest standing building on Merseyside.

EDWARD I (1239–1307) was King of England, known to his admirers as the "Hammer of the Scots" in the days when the two countries were at almost constant war with each other. On at least two occasions, he visited Birkenhead Priory, where Benedictine friars had already started rowing merchants and others across the river to the fishing village of Liverpool. He saw Birkenhead as an ideal spot for assembling forces, which could be used to further his ambitions in Wales and Ireland.

EDWARD II (1284–1327) was King of England from 1307. Although big and strong, he lacked intellect and determination, leaving difficult decisions to favourites of whom he was too fond. His army was utterly routed by Robert the Bruce's Scots at Bannockburn in 1314, a victory that would eventually win a resurgent Scotland independence from England. In 1318, he issued a licence, which enabled the monks at Birkenhead Priory to offer hospitality to travellers. He visited the priory six years later and was taken by the ferrymen to Ince.

This must have been a happy interlude in his reign, which was for the most part marred by pestilence and war. Despite his own sexual inclinations, he had married the beautiful Isabella. Her brother was Charles IV of France, who seized the English territories there. Edward sent Isabella across the channel to intervene. The ensuing events are perhaps one of the most painful examples of what happens when a woman is scorned. Isabella and her followers soon arrived at the coast of Suffolk, where they gathered a considerable force. Edward abdicated and was imprisoned in Berkeley Castle in Wales. There he suffered a dreadful death featuring his bottom and a red-hot poker. Isabella's son, also Edward, replaced him as king.

EDWARD III (1312–1377) was a great King of England, who restored authority to the realm after the disastrous reign of his father. In 1330, he granted the charter formally recognising the right of the monks at Birkenhead Priory to run the Mersey ferries.

JAMES ATHERTON (1770–1838) was a Liverpool businessman and builder responsible for the development of New Brighton as a resort. He also instigated the building of St George's Church, Everton, known locally as the Iron Church because of its cast-iron interior.

NORMAN KINGHAM (1921–2006), architect, businessman and former owner of Fort Perch Rock, New Brighton.

DOUG AND ALICE DARROCH and their children, owners of Fort Perch Rock, New Brighton.

TOM MURPHY (1949–). On the Georgian wood of a floor in a house in a district of old Liverpool, where gentlemen with pork-chop whiskers once plotted business deals, there stands a tall figure, whose dark hair has turned white, but whose eyes still carry the vivid blue quizzicality of his Irish ancestry.

He plays classical music on a gramophone that looks antique, but is really modern, being fitted with all the gadgets necessary for tapes and CDs, as well as old-fashioned records. From the music he finds the mood for the men and women he makes. For in Liverpool, after God, Tom Murphy is the most prolific maker of men and women.

No sooner are you through this sculptor's front door than there to greet you is the demurely smiling Princess Diana (1961–1997, estranged wife of Prince Charles and the self-styled Queen of Hearts), looking rather elegant.

The five-foot fibreglass statue of this clay model was commissioned for a shopping centre in Colwyn Bay.

People appreciated Princess Diana's many visits to Merseyside, always calling her Lady Diana, as she had been before her unhappy marriage to Prince Charles. She had a natural affinity with those struggling against life's difficulties, whether through disability, poverty, sorrow or inclination. This quality appealed to many in Liverpool, where people only dislike the highborn if they have lofty manners. Emotional affinity counts for more than the class difference. Anyway, Tom has sculpted many great people from all classes.

The full sized ones with their locations and the dates of their instalment include Harold Wilson, Prime Minister and MP for Huyton, Huyton town centre, Knowsley, 2006; Noel Chavasse, Great War doctor awarded the MC and double VC for treating the wounded under fire, Abercromby Square, Liverpool, 2008; Johnnie Walker, hero of the Battle of the Atlantic, Liverpool Pier Head, 1994; Billy Fury, rock and roller, Albert Dock, Liverpool, 2003; Sir John and Cecil Moores, businessmen, Old Hall, Hall Street, Liverpool, 1996; Henry Cotton (1929–1993, first Chancellor of Liverpool John Moores University 1992–1993), at the university, 1999; John Lennon, Beatle, Liverpool Airport, 2002; Bill Shankly, football manager, Anfield, 1997; William Ralph (Dixie) Dean, footballer, outside Goodison Park, 2001; the Blitz Memorial, Liverpool Pier Head, 2000; Princess Diana, Liverpool Women's Hospital, 1997, in addition to the one in Colwyn Bay; and Ken Dodd, comedian, and Bessie Braddock, politician, together at Lime Street station, Liverpool, 2009.

In 1988 Tom's paintings won the BBC North West Art competition. Despite the accolade, he felt that he could achieve more through sculpture.

And he has given us a fine crop of full-sized statues to prove his point, but he has also sculpted smaller figures of other prominent people, including all The Beatles and George Best (1946–2005), the superb Northern Ireland and Manchester United footballer.

Tom, the artist, is a man of experience. In the style much admired by Liverpudlians, he taught himself how to paint and to sculpt from what he had learned in a roller-coasting life. This has taken him down the pits near St Helens, across the seas as a merchant sailor and into shops, where he unfurled his charm as a salesman. For three years he worked in the Community College on Myrtle Street, Liverpool, teaching art to people with learning difficulties.

All this makes him a champion and a symbol of hope to those who have the passion to express themselves, but feel inhibited because they didn't go to college or university. That may sound old-fashioned but such fears still hold people back. You can have letters springing after your name or you can populate the streets with immortal men and women made of bronze and a little of your own sweat. Tom chose the second course. So, for many, he represents the triumph of the individual, unafraid to go his own way.

One morning we were talking around mugs of tea brewed to perfection. Tom referred in passing to a conversation he had with Adrian Henri years ago. At the time Tom was an emerging artist beginning to win commissions. Adrian, though a fine painter himself, was long established as a "darling" to those who creep down the aisles of our art galleries – the purring aesthetes in denim, leaning their heads this way and that way to better appreciate the works hanging before them.

Anyway, Adrian and Tom began talking about the Holy Ghost Parochial Social Club in Bootle. Now there are people, mostly strangers, who would feel that was a strange sort of name for a social club, but when you have lived around here for a while, you learn to accept such things, in much the same way as other people talk about meetings in the car park outside Sainsbury's. Anyway, little of importance came from the conversation, other than the fact that Tom preferred neo-classical art, while Adrian favoured more abstract works, though they both accepted a little of the other's opinion.

What amazes me about Tom, after all these years, is that he's still such an unhurried fellow. It can take him months to complete a statue to his satisfaction, or as close as an artist will ever get to that elusive ambition. It often takes even longer to deal with the commissioning committees, but he rarely loses his cool demeanour or expresses frustration, even when some brainless and soulless bureaucrat asks him to move a wonderful sculpture from its station on the pavement, as though it was of little more importance than a tub for flowers or a litterbin.

On the big days, when his work is unveiled, Tom always looks smart in a conventional dark suit and a white shirt and tie. In this respect, he is the very antithesis of the later generation of artists, who offered us their unmade beds and pickled sheep, in the hope of persuading us that they had talent and vision.

Tom has respect for people. He knows that Harold Wilson had his detractors, but he was also a man of generosity, wit and intellect, possessing a remarkable memory. Johnnie Walker and Noel Chavasse carried out deeds of bravery beyond the imaginings of most of us. To give them immortality in the city of their renown is an awesome responsibility.

Tom stood by widow Yoko Ono when the statue of her husband John Lennon was unveiled at Liverpool Airport, watched by Cherie Blair, wife of the then prime minister, Tony Blair. Later in 2002 the Queen inspected the towering Lennon when she opened a new terminal at the airport.

Such moments mean a great deal to Tom, who left St Aloysius School, Huyton, when he was 15, and Merseybeat was edging through. Like so many other young chaps, Tom was a drummer and also guitarist with natural comedic leanings, which enabled him to play in a couple of entertaining groups with considerable success, though never approaching the big-time. He was a free spirit, who had hitchhiked to Rome soon after leaving school. But playing in a group didn't seem to offer a great future, so he sold the drum-kit to pay for a uniform to go to sea, working in shops before that. In fact, groups were to gain in strength for several more years. Such is life. Tom just gets on with it.

"I was walking past NEMS (famous Liverpool record shop) and I saw Billy Fury walking along, I didn't immediately recognise him as the star, but just as somebody I knew," remembered Tom. "At the time, he seemed like a dated pop star, but he wasn't really. It was just that he was a bit older than the Liverpool groups of the day. I was with somebody else and I looked at Billy when we walked past and he looked at me and there was this strange spark of something, which I have learned to recognise now. It is almost like jumping through time because, of course, I did this sculpture of him and I ended up looking at his face endlessly.

"I had the same sort of feeling about Ken Dodd. I might have only been about 15. I saw him getting off the train and walking through the station. I remember thinking he looked very pale and tired. I had this strange feeling about him as well. Maybe it is just because he was famous, but there was something more than that. I followed him round with a tape measure after that," he added.

Obviously that is not literally true, but if you are in Tom's company for any time, you will become aware that he is studying your features and wondering how you would look in stone.

"I absolutely love doing sculptures," he said. "When you love doing something, work is something that you really look forward to. My first statue was John Lennon. At the time I had been working with people with learning difficulties in Widnes. Out of boredom one day, I made this giant pair of legs out of wood. I could see John Lennon in the legs. I had this fidgetiness at the time. I was always wanting to make something. When I made that John Lennon (on which the one at the airport would be based), I felt absolutely confident that it would be okay. I have never suffered with a lack of confidence making sculptures. Everything is a work in progress."

That's the way the man thinks about life after giving a kind of immortality to our rock stars, heroes and politicians.

BILL SHANKLY (1913–1981). To Liverpool fans, he was the Messiah and his stance with arms outstretched, as shown in Tom Murphy's sculpture, is the image he leaves on Earth – the man who gave himself to football and those fans. That is the most important part of his life, but the "raw" facts are impressive as well.

He was one of 10 children born in Glenbuck, a mining community in

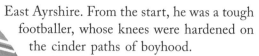

East Ayrshire. From the start, he was a tough footballer, whose knees were hardened on the cinder paths of boyhood.

His English playing career, as an unyielding wing-half, was with Carlisle United (1932–1933, 16 appearances) and Preston North End (1933–1949, 297 appearances). He also played five times for Scotland, but the Second World War interrupted his career. Until being appointed Liverpool's manager in 1959, he had managed unglamorous clubs – Carlisle, Grimsby, Workington and the sadly faded Huddersfield.

But his Liverpool were Second Division champions, 1962; First Division champions, 1964; FA Cup winners, 1965; First Division Champions and European Cup Winners' Cup runners-up, 1966; First Division runners-up 1969; FA Cup runners-up, 1971; First Division champions and UEFA Cup winners, 1973; FA Cup winners and First Division runners-up, 1974.

He retired in 1974 and was appointed OBE. Shankly's passion was for the working man. His voice was flinted in another age and pitched to the crunch of coal dust. To those outside Liverpool's football fraternity, he was a rough-hewn philosopher with a rasping wit, on whose emery hair you could have struck a match. He possessed a direct generosity, but it was reserved for those whom he identified as belonging to his kind. He would not have had any sympathy for the agents, marketing men and the prawn-sandwich nibblers, who have helped finance the game in the twenty-first century.

When the barber asked him what he wanted off the top, Shankly replied "Everton". This quip raised his status in a city, where comedians are cherished. His observation that football was not a matter of life and death, but more important than that, appealed to the growing number of fans drawn from the colleges and universities. Such thoughts were printed in the posh papers, whose football and ballet correspondents sometimes seemed inter-changeable.

People loved the idea of their game attracting intellectuals. Backed by this reputation, Shankly was able to broadcast with some success on local radio. However, my few conversations with him tended to be strained, as he spotted straightaway that I was not cut from his granite.

In the early 1970s, it was reported that Shankly had told his players to marry only at the end of the season because marriage sapped the energy, which should be stored for the much more important pursuit of football. The old *Daily Sketch*, a national paper that was soon to cease publication, asked me to check this out. That particular telephone discussion was cut short by his decision to hang up. Shankly was quite right. You have to remember that was a different age, before footballers stepped out with models, movie stars and pop singers. Even then, though, there were glamorous young players who would not have restricted their sexual activities to a spot of slap and tickle with the wife out of season.

Shankly will always be the voice of the working man in the Kop, for whom football was not a hobby or a game, but a religion with its own hymns, creed and prophets. More than anything, he believed that a tough upbringing made men out of boys. Boxers, comedians and footballers were the people with whom he could most readily identify. Such men rose to strength from hardship. He would not have said this himself, but underpinning his thoughts was the Darwinian notion of the survival of the fittest. However, the fittest on the football field could often be the runt – those blessed wee Scots with the pinched faces and the big hearts, whose superlative dribbling and natural cunning could floor the big boys.

HAROLD WILSON (1916–1995). With his heavily pouched eyes and school-masterly hair, this was a man who could sit on a striped deckchair in a pair of cream shorts and cross his legs, allowing everyone to see that he wore socks under his sandals.

Harold Wilson was the Everyman of British politics, who doused his fish with HP sauce, but the smoke from his pipe was a screen. Behind it, there was a brilliant mind. He was a wit and intellectual with the common touch, who preferred in private to puff on a cigar. But Wilson would never have wanted to be seen in public as a toff, a mini Churchill in need of a war to build his reputation.

Wilson's reputation now is not particularly high, though he won four of the five elections he fought as Labour leader – in 1964, 1966, February 1974 and October 1974, losing to Edward Heath's Conservatives in 1970. In 1976, he retired as an exhausted man, perhaps already sensing that his remarkable powers were waning.

Wilson didn't succeed in his grand ambition of making Labour the natural party of government. Margaret Thatcher led the Conservatives to victory in 1979. But Wilson did at least help to hold the party together during times of industrial strife and massive social changes. To many of us, though, he did something even more important. He gave a human face to the highest office in the land.

There was something of the music hall comic in his manner and he was blessed with perfect comedic delivery. He seemed in touch with the young people of the 1960s, while also having the gentle outlook of the English bloke, occasionally stirred into waspish retaliation.

Tom Murphy with Tony and Cherie Blair and
Harold Wilson's widow, Mary (Baroness Wilson of Rievaulx)
© TOM MURPHY

Snobs on the posh papers called Wilson "lower" middle-class, which then
was about the most stinging insult available. In truth, he was just middle-
class, though he had the widely practised skill of shading his accent to suit
those around him. Wilson's father, Herbert, was an industrial chemist and
Liberal. His mother Ethel (née Seddon) had trained as a schoolteacher before
marriage.

Wilson spent his childhood in Huddersfield, where he passed the 11-plus
into grammar school. When his father lost his job in Yorkshire, the family
settled in Bebington, Wirral. Harold attended Wirral Grammar School for
Boys. His prowess as a cross-country runner, combined with his academic
gifts, led to him being appointed head boy. He advanced to Jesus College,
Cambridge, studying Modern History and then Philosophy, Politics and
Economics. He became an Oxford don aged 21. Wilson was elected to
Parliament as the member of Ormskirk in the Labour landslide of 1945.

The rearrangement of constituency boundaries led to him narrowly winning
Huyton in the General Election of 1950. He would represent that seat until he
left the House of Commons in 1983, before being elevated to Baron Wilson
of Rievaulx (the name of an abbey in north Yorkshire).

Some left-wing trade unionists on Merseyside believed that Wilson had
betrayed their cause with his desire to curb shop-floor power and modernise
many of Britain's lamentably dated production methods, but generally

he remained popular in Liverpool and he was a fine and conscientious constituency MP.

Thinking about his career all these years later, I can't recall any other politician, who is so remembered for image, rather than substance. There is no doubt he was an opportunist, as was demonstrated by his decision to award The Beatles the MBE in 1965.

Perhaps more than anything, though, he will be remembered for Mrs Wilson's Diary in *Private Eye* magazine – a superbly crafted spoof on the domestic life he had as prime minister with his charming, if diffident, wife Mary, a poet of considerable talent in the women's magazine tradition. Yet, to be remembered as a decent English bloke is not such a bad thing. Tom Murphy's statue of him in Huyton town centre captures that spirit.

NOEL CHAVASSE (1884–1917) possessed a rare bravery and a respect for his fellow man, which symbolised the bloom of British youth lost amid the poppy fields of the Great War. In this representation of noble sacrifice, he far surpasses the poet Rupert Brooke (1887–1915), who was immortalised by his sentiment in *The Soldier* – "If I should die think only this of me: That there is a corner of a foreign field that is forever England."

Chavasse has his corner.

Brooke, who gave words to the ideal, died from septicaemia after being bitten by a mosquito off the coast of Greece before he could see active service – unlike Chavasse, who would be awarded the MC and two VCs (one posthumously) for his gallantry as a doctor treating wounded soldiers. If it had not been for the war, people from less privileged backgrounds would have seen Chavasse and his twin brother, Christopher, as lucky young men. But the war changed everything.

Their father, Francis James Chavasse and their mother, Edith Jane Chavasse (née Maude), came to Liverpool from Oxford when he was appointed the city's Anglican bishop in 1900. Four years later, Edward VII and Queen Alexandria laid the foundation stone for Liverpool Cathedral. Noel and Christopher, who was 20 minutes older, both attended Liverpool College, the public school that educated the sons of the city's merchant and professional classes.

The twins excelled at all sports and also did well at their lessons. Noel went to Trinity College, Oxford, where he received Blues in rugby and lacrosse. Christopher also went to Trinity College. In 1908, they took part in the Summer Olympics in London. Christopher came second in his heat for the 400 metres. Noel was third in his heat for the same event. Neither qualified for the semi-finals, but that was a minor setback on their glittering paths. Then came that war.

Christopher became an Army Chaplain. Noel was attached to the Liverpool Scottish Battalion of the King's regiment. He was awarded the MC for treating the wounded in No Man's Land during the Battle of Hooge on June

16, 1916, a day never to be forgotten by the Liverpool Scottish. In their attack on Bellewaarde Ridge, four officers and 75 other ranks were killed, 11 officers and 201 men were wounded, six officers and 103 men were reported missing (all the officers and most of those men were in fact dead).

The following year Noel Chavasse was awarded his first VC for treating 20 men at Guillemont on the Somme. From July 31 to August 2, Chavasse refused to leave his post, though grievously wounded. Time and time again, in mounting desperation, he faced heavy gunfire to haul wounded men to comparative safety. But he was exhausted and he had lost too much blood. Noel Chavasse, the most decorated British serviceman of the war, died from his wounds soon afterwards and was buried at the cemetery in Brandhoek, near the ambulance base, where he had been working – not knowing that his twin, Christopher, serving with the ninth Army Corps had also been wounded and awarded the MC and the Croix de Guerre for gallantry in another theatre of war.

Christopher later became the Bishop of Rochester. He died in 1962. Their younger brother, Francis Bernard (1889–1941), also a doctor, received the MC in 1916 and went on to become a distinguished eye surgeon.

His younger brother, Aidan (1892–1917) was killed leading a reconnaissance patrol. Aidan's body was never found and his name is listed on the Menin Gate at Ypres.

Both the younger brothers also attended Liverpool College. Their eldest sister, Dorothea Chavasse, was involved in charitable work for the war effort and their twin sisters, Edith and Mary, were both nurses.

Tom Murphy's statue to Noel Chavasse, which is also dedicated to 15 other Liverpool VCs is situated near the family's old home in Abercromby Square, Liverpool.

"It is a trinity," said Tom. "You have Chavasse dragging a wounded soldier, helped by a stretcher-bearer. I wanted a design, which is like a wave, as though they are marching on in eternity. The battle never finishes for those who died. They are always locked in that field. It is where all those young men were cut off in the prime of life. The wounded soldier is a Christian image, like taking Christ off the Cross. Of course, Noel Chavasse was a Christian."

He was also a Great Liverpudlian.

*Here are the other 15 Liverpool VCs: John Kirk (1827–1865), Indian Mutiny; Charles Anderson (1826–1899), Indian Mutiny; William Connolly (1817–1891), Indian Mutiny; Frederick Whirlpool (1829–1899), Indian Mutiny; Alfred Stowell Jones (1832–1920), Indian Mutiny; George Hinckley (1819–1904), Second China War; Paul Aloysius Kenna (1862–1915), Egypt; Ernest Wright Alexander (1870–1934), Great War; William Ratcliffe (1882–1963), Great War; Cyril Edward Gourley (1893–1982), Great War; Gabriel George Coury (1896–1956), Great War; David Jones (1892–1916), Great War; Albert White (1889–1917), Great War; Ronald Neil Stuart (1886–1954), Great War; and Hugh McDonald McKenzie (1885–1917), Great War.

CAPTAIN JOHN (JOHNNIE) WALKER DSO (1896–1944).

The Battle of the Atlantic ran for the duration of the Second World War, starting on September 3, 1939 (the day war broke out), with the sinking of the passenger line, SS *Athenia*. The Allies conducted the war from the Western Approaches' HQ in Liverpool. By the end of the war in Europe in May 1945, the battle had cost the lives of 30, 248 of our sailors; 3,500 merchant ships and 175 warships had been sunk. Some 28,000 German sailors were killed and 783 Axis submarines were sunk. From our side, the outstanding figure was "Johnnie" Walker, whose nickname was taken from a popular brand of whisky. His statue, sculpted by Tom Murphy, stands at the Pier Head.

Walker was born in Plymouth and emerged as top in his class from the Royal Navy College at Dartmouth. He seemed destined for a swift advance to a high position in the Royal Navy. The young man certainly had the ability, but he was also self-willed and inclined to embrace unconventional ideas, not a quality admired by the top brass in the Senior Service in peacetime. Walker had served in the Great War with distinction, but he had noticed with increasing concern that the German U-boats (submarines) were an extremely effective weapon in destroying the shipping on which we, as an island race, depended. If hostilities ever broke out again between Britain and Germany, the U-boats would play an important part in the outcome. Sadly, Walker's opinions on this were of no particular interest to those who failed to understand Hitler's ambition.

The Second World War changed everyone's thinking. Although most of the early news was bad, promoting a sense of German invincibility in the minds of pessimists, our morale was lifted by a peculiarly British episode. With France falling fast and our expeditionary force in full retreat, the Allies decided on an evacuation from the beach at Dunkirk. Much helped by an armada of small craft, which crossed the English Channel in late May and early June 1940, we were able to bring almost 340,000 Allied troops to Britain and they would serve in other theatres of war. Historians have never fully understood why Hitler allowed this to happen. It mattered not. For propaganda purposes we had the "Miracle of Deliverance".

Walker had done his bit at Dunkirk, but he was more concerned about the menace of German submarines. Germany's purpose in the Battle of the Atlantic was simply to starve Britain while limiting the supply of essential goods being shipped to our allies in the USSR. Conditions were appalling on the Russian convoys. The drips froze on the ends of the sailors' noses and ungloved hands would freeze on the ships' railings. To be sunk in such conditions was a nightmare beyond description.

The building in Derby Square, Liverpool, became our Battle of the Atlantic HQ in 1941. Walker was based at the Gladstone Dock. At this time, Britain and Canada maintained 400 escort ships along the Atlantic convoy routes. But the U-boats were having it practically all their own way. A nation, which had traded with the world for so long, became almost entirely dependent on home production. Walker had under his command an escort group of two sloops and seven corvettes. The conventional wisdom was that the escorts should remain close to the ships that they were protecting. Walker believed a more aggressive policy would work better. The U-boats should be hunted and destroyed.

On his first convoy, between England and Gibraltar, he sank three U-boats in 10 days, sinking four more on the return trip. Yet, there was still some scepticism about Walker's methods. Crucially, however, he gained the support of Admiral Sir Max Horton, the commander-in-chief of Western Approaches, who gave the go-ahead for Walker's idea of freeing six, well-equipped, fast sloops to hunt the U-boats, wherever they should be. So, from the bridge of his own sloop, *Starling*, Walker trained the crews on *Cygnet*, *Wild Goose*, *Wren*, *Woodpecker* and *Kite*. By following his instructions, they matched the U-boats.

We could not claim to have won the Battle of the Atlantic. The U-boats remained a menace to the very end of the war, but thousands of men lived and untold quantities of cargo reached their destinations because of his actions.

On July 7, 1944, when the Allies were advancing through Normandy, Walker suffered a fatal cerebral thrombosis. But still he stands at the Liverpool Pier Head, salted by the spray, as he considers the mood of the sea.

JOHN MOORES (1896–1993). It is unusual for a rich businessman to be revered by his staff and customers. But John Moores was different. He was a dream-maker, who rose to prominence during the 1920s and 1930s, when millions of Britons lived in dire poverty. For many people hope lay with the trade unions and the emerging Labour Party, both of which campaigned to improve the conditions of working men and women. As one of eight children born in Eccles, near Salford, to John Moores, a bricklayer, and his wife, Louisa, a mill worker, young John appreciated the promise of instant wealth.

After leaving school, Moores trained with the Post Office as a telegraphist, joining the Commercial Cable Company in 1912. During the Great War, he served as wireless operator in Aberdeen, before returning to the cable company, working for a while in Ireland, where he started some enterprises of his own.

In the early 1920s, John Jervis Bernard from Birmingham had begun a football pool. The idea was simple. Punters would bet on the outcome of matches and the winnings would be paid from the resulting "pool". Management took its slice for bearing the initial cost of distributing the coupons. It was a fine idea, but it would only work if large numbers joined. Moores and two pals, Colin Askham and Bill Hughes, had a similar idea. Each invested £50 to launch it. The first 4,000 coupons were distributed outside Manchester United's Old Trafford ground. The results were disappointing, so the trio printed 10,000 for a match in Hull. They also need a catchy name. Askham had been orphaned and adopted by an aunt. His birth name had been Colin Henry Littlewood.

The partners decided to call their enterprise the Littlewoods Pool Company. It didn't help much. In the season 1924/1925, Moores, who had an office in Church Street, Liverpool, bought out his partners for £200 each.

His decision to keep faith with the idea paid dividends and, by promising to make others rich, he became very rich himself. Every week there were winners and the stories of the biggest ones were featured in the newspapers.

In 1932, John started the Littlewoods Mail order division and that was followed in 1937 by the opening in Blackpool of their first department store.

In 1932, John's younger brother Cecil (1902–1989), who was a wizard with figures, had been appointed chairman of the pools division, a position that he would hold until 1979.

Every Saturday evening millions of Britons sat by their wirelesses, and later the TV, with pens poised, checking on the numbers of score draws they had on their coupons. For those few minutes of dreaming everyone could be a millionaire. Of course, John and Cecil won the pools every week.

In 1960 John became chairman of Everton, a football club with a glorious past but an indifferent present. His money transformed its fortunes. His decision to sack the popular manager, Johnny Carey, in the back of a taxi cab sparked anger and resentment, which was forgotten when his replacement, Harry Catterick, led Everton to the First Division championship in 1963. Moores was chairman of the club until 1965 and again between 1968 and 1973. Everton won the championship in 1970.

John Moores was knighted in 1980 – recognition for his patronage of the arts and his unfailing conviction that his staff should be treated well. He was very keen that Littlewoods staff should see themselves as part of an extended family. Pay and conditions were comparatively good and social events, such as the lavish Miss Littlewoods competition, fostered a happy spirit. John Moores started his contemporary painting prize exhibition in 1957.

He and Cecil had offered millions of people a dream and for a few it came true. Tom Murphy's statue of the brothers stands on Old Hall Street, Liverpool.

BILLY FURY (1940–1983). There was a pop impresario called Larry Parnes who had a special gift. He saw young men in the same way as adolescent girls did. It made him a lot of money. Now Birkenhead was a rock and roll town. The tough-looking young men there liked the American style. Some of them had gathered in the sumptuous, art deco interior of the Essoldo Ritz cinema, where the red carpet was as thick as the soles on their brothel-creeper shoes. Also in there was Parnes.

Espresso coffee machines hissed in the steamy cafés. Pigeons pecked in the grand square near the railway station. Gulls bickered and spread their wings over the towering cranes. Girls pouted and reflected their freshly rouged lips in little mirrors. Teddy boys combed their hair in shop windows. But the fair hair was already piled high and perfectly sculpted over the unforgettable face of the slight boy with clothes-hanger shoulders, who was approaching the stage door on this famous day of October 1, 1958.

Parnes (1930–1989) was holding his Rock and Roll Extravaganza at the picture palace. Included on the bill were Marty Wilde and the Wildcats, Vince Eager, the John Barry Seven and a cheeky comedian named Jimmy Tarbuck. But the fair boy standing at the stage door in the gabardine coat had sent Parnes a tape of his own singing, but he hadn't yet had the courtesy of a reply. Here was a sensitive chap, hardened by his life as a tug boatman, who wrote songs.

His name was Ronnie Wycherley. Eager and Brian Bennett, then the drummer with the Wildcats, who went on to play with Cliff Richard and the Shadows, met him at the stage door.

They introduced him to Parnes, who suggested that Ronnie should sing in one of the dressing rooms. Ronnie performed his own songs, Maybe Tomorrow and Margo, strumming the melodies on a Hofner Committee guitar, belonging to Kenny Packwood of the Wildcats. The special instinct was strong in Parnes in those minutes and he booked Ronnie for that night's show.

Girls went mad; Billy Fury was born. It was Parnes's habit to name his boys after a characteristic he admired in them – hence Vince Eager, Duffy Power, Marty Wilde, Dickie Pride, Johnny Gentle and then Billy Fury. Despite his new name, Billy was a shy man, who loved the quiet of the country. It was only on stage that he seemed untamed, living up to his billing – strutting and posing and hunching his shoulders in suggestive poses, which the girls loved. It was a fine combination, the wild man with a poetic heart. His image was far closer to that of the Americans, such as Elvis, Eddie Cochran and Gene Vincent, than the early British rock and rollers, who seemed to be groomed for the summer shows like the music hall acts of an earlier generation.

Billy was born into a loving family in Liverpool's Dingle district. His father, Albert, was a cobbler. His mother, Jean, remains a dedicated fan, as does his brother, Albie Wycherley, also a pop singer, who performs under the name of Jason Eddie.

Despite the rheumatic fever, which weakened his heart valves, Billy was an active enough boy at Wellington Road School, Toxteth, but he was easily diverted from his studies by the rock and roll craze. It is strange to think that such music is now taught in schools, but the old-fashioned schoolmasters did not approve at all. The preachers in their pulpits were calling it the Devil's music, though, strangely, many of its disciples were happy to call themselves Christians.

At home, Billy had learned to play the guitar and piano. He left school at 15 and took a job as a tugman with the Alexandra Towing Company. His natural good looks and slightly mysterious manner appealed greatly to girls and, once he was a star, they came, screaming, to besiege his family's house.

Billy's hits started in 1959 with Maybe Tomorrow (which reached 18 in the charts). There followed *Margo* (28), *Colette* (9), *Wondrous Place* (25), *Halfway to Paradise* (3) *Jealousy* (2), *Last Night Was Made for Love* (4), *It's Only Make Believe* (10) and *In Thoughts of You* (9). His last hit was *Give Me Your Word*, which made the Top 30 in 1967. But he is now just as fondly remembered for his 1960 LP of 10 self-penned songs, *The Sound of Fury*. Success with your own compositions was an ideal that would be followed by his fellow Great Liverpudlians, Paul McCartney and John Lennon.

His appearance, with David Essex, Keith Moon and Ringo Starr in Ray Connolly's 1973 holiday camp film, *That'll Be the Day*, was a reminder of the old days. Fury plays the aptly named Stormy Tempest.

By the end of his career as a major star, Billy was suffering from what would prove to be terminal heart problems, bringing great sorrow to his family and his fans. The Press called him the "British Elvis" but Billy was an original and he retains the devotion of a huge fan club. His voice was essentially a light baritone, though lacking the range or mellow tone of Elvis's. But there is an earthy and sympathetic quality in many of his recordings. His interpretation of *Wondrous Place* is superb. This was a man who could name all the birds in the sky and thrill the girls with his stance behind the microphone. Hardly a day goes by when his records are not played on local radio. His statue, sculpted by Tom Murphy, stands at the Albert Dock, where he can hear the gulls and the ceaseless lap of the river, as he did as a boy.

KEN DODD (1927–).

Think for a moment of the great men and women who have dedicated their lives to a noble cause – the soldiers, the healers, the missionaries, the inventors, the writers, the composers and perhaps even the politicians. Now think of this man. He has been more dedicated to his cause than any of them. That cause, of course, is making us laugh. But I also think of his courage.

In a sense he has the courage of all the comedians, who can stand on a little stage in front of rows and rows of people, shielded only by jokes and stories. But they have always been enough for him.

Ken Dodd is loved as the last of the old-style comedians, a man who can reach back to the music halls. In private moments, he will talk seriously of his devotion to comedy. This is his subject and he has studied its masters, having himself taken copious notes about what will make people laugh. He knows that a story, which will have them rubbing their tummies in Scunthorpe, will meet a blank stare in Cheltenham.

In public moments, though, and these are the

moments that really count in his extraordinary life, Ken has turned a feather-duster, this gloriously politically incorrect tickling stick, into a symbol of old England, as potent in its vivid colours as is Britannia in her steady dignity.

Journalists and authors have tried to pry behind the mask – perhaps to see the tears of a clown, but nothing is revealed. But we know that Doddy is the embodiment of England's comedic tradition – from the court jester to the wide-eyed satirist, never quite crossing the threshold into our new society, the cold, technological age. He has played most of our theatres – before the eyes of children and toothless grannies, gumming along to the songs beneath the Grecian pillars and those grand galleries, sculpted with swags of fruit and full-bosomed maidens. But he also raised mirth in the weary old halls of seaside towns, standing forlorn by the neon arcades with their one-armed bandits and teasing push-the-penny machines.

Ken Dodd's job has been to give happiness to others and he has done that – producing laughter by the mountain and rolling it down the generations. Pounding within him, there is a rare generosity of spirit. But he is also a genius. Comic understanding dances down his genes. How else would you eat tomatoes through a tennis racquet or introduce Professor Rufus Chuckabutty to strangers?

It is a shame that many modern critics have been concerned only about how long he is on stage – often four or five hours – rather than why he is on stage. But watching him there, you see an old man, who miraculously rejuvenates as his act progresses.

Dodd was born in Thomas Lane, in the quaintly named Knotty Ash, Liverpool, and that has remained his home. His father, Arthur, was a coal merchant, but he was also a saxophonist, who had played in orchestras. His mother, Sarah, was a pianist, when not collecting the money from the coal rounds. Their son was a natural entertainer, putting on Punch and Judy shows and performing as a ventriloquist in his garden, when he was still a pupil at Knotty Ash Primary School. He also sang in the local St John's Church Choir.

Ken became a splendid tenor, whose records held high positions in the charts. Had he not been such a great comedian, he could have made a fine living simply as a singer with a near-operatic voice, which was heard on his big hits of the 1960s – *Love is Like a Violin*, *Still*, *Happiness*, *Tears* (a British number one for six weeks), *Promises* and many others, often in the sentimental style.

Although his songs suggest the sorrow of the funny man, it is not a side of his character ever displayed in public, except perhaps before Liverpool Crown Court in 1988, where he was cleared of charges brought by the Inland Revenue. Inevitably gags about his dealings with the taxman were included in his routine.

The details of Ken's show business career are well known. After leaving

Holt High School at 14, he joined his father's business, learning to drive a lorry, but after a mishap with a pothole, the young man branched out into sales, flogging bleach, soap and firelighters from door to door. But, throughout this time, he was developing his act in local hotels and halls and continuing to read extensively, particularly from the master of comic writing, P.G. Wodehouse.

Ken joined a concert party and after being spotted performing at the New Brighton Tivoli, he made his professional debut as a singer/comedian at the Nottingham Empire in 1954. He was soon appearing on radio and TV, where he hooked up with the Liverpool scriptwriter Eddie Braben (born 1930). But it was his appearances at all the top theatres that sustained his reputation. In 1971, he played Malvolio in a production of Shakespeare's *Twelfth Night* at the Liverpool Playhouse.

He continues to appear in the theatres, offering his gift to others. My feeling is that Ken is the most popular of all the Great Liverpudlians.

In June 2009, Tom Murphy's statue of Ken and Bessie Braddock, reaching towards each other in mutual admiration, was unveiled at Liverpool's Lime Street railway station. It is called Chance Meeting.

ELIZABETH MARGARET "BESSIE" BRADDOCK (1899–1970) was a Socialist politician, who had a magnificent, indomitable face, with jowls quivering in indignation and small eyes burning like coals. She carried it, and all the passion it expressed, on a body that seemed accustomed to absorbing potatoes and squeezing the washing through a mangle.

Bessie, often prefixed with "Our" to emphasise her place among ordinary people, was the daughter of Mary "Ma" Bamber, a well-known political activist in Liverpool. Bessie was brought up on Zante Street and was first attracted to the Communist Party, but soon felt that social justice would be achieved quicker in the more democratic Labour Party, which would also serve her own desire for advancement.

In 1922 she married another committed Socialist, Jack Braddock (1893–1963), who would become leader of Liverpool City Council (from 1955 to 1961 and again in 1963). In many ways he was the more adroit political operator, but she had the image and the populist instincts. Her enthusiasm for football, popular music and boxing all helped draw people to the cause.

Bessie became a councillor in 1930, serving St Anne's ward. She was a member of the Union of Shop, Distributive and Allied Workers, which had a high percentage of female members. During the war she worked for the ambulance service.

It was as an MP that she won her greatest renown, winning the Liverpool Exchange constituency during the 1945 Labour landslide. In those days, men, even on the Labour benches, were from privileged backgrounds, and dominated the House of Commons. "Battling Bessie", therefore, was something of a novelty, whose simple desire to improve the living standards of working-class people, was lost in the coarse caricature presented by the Tory Press. Even so, she became a member of the Labour Party's National Executive and was vice-chairman of the Labour Party in 1968. She was granted the Freedom of Liverpool in 1970.

Although canny and sometimes self-promoting, Bessie upheld the values of another age when life was very much harder. In June 2009, Tom Murphy's statue of her and Ken Dodd was unveiled at Liverpool's Lime Street railway station, introducing her to a new generation. Older people were surprised by the coupling of the staunch Socialist and the comedian known for his Conservative sympathies.

"I see Bessie Braddock as part of the 1940s and 1950s, that dull grey period that followed the war," Tom told me. "When I was growing up, life was very black and white. It felt like that until the 1960s when someone turned the colour on. Everyone had the same things. If someone had a new sofa, it was like they had won the pools.

"Bessie Braddock was someone that your parents and everyone admired. She was a people's champion. She was loved. Bessie thought Ken was hilarious and used to go to his shows. She took Harold Wilson and his wife (Mary), to them.

"Ken is a Conservative supporter and she was Labour through and through, but these things break down before the greater thing of being two Scousers. In Bessie's face, I see a woman, who has got intelligence and compassion. She has a look of Liverpool humour, definitely. In Liverpool you can't survive without a sense of humour. She is not a beauty, but I find beauty in every face. Like her, Ken learned his trade on the streets. She was the greatest Liverpool politician of her generation and he remains the greatest comedian."

JAMES GILLESPIE GRAHAM (1776–1855) was an architect born in Dunblane and associated with the Scottish baronial style. He designed Hamilton Square in Birkenhead.

WILLIAM LAIRD (1780–1841) was born in Greenock, near Glasgow. In 1810 he moved the Liverpool to work in his family's rope factory. He began the Birkenhead Iron Works in 1924. It later developed into the shipyard, which became Cammell Laird. He bought land on a plateau above the river and hired the architect James Gillespie Graham to design and lay out Hamilton Square.

JOHN LAIRD (1805–1874) was responsible for the development of his father's Birkenhead Iron Works into the shipyard, which eventually became Cammell Laird. He was educated at the Liverpool Royal Institution and trained as a solicitor. He was responsible for advances in the use of iron sheeting in ships. This would be riveted together in much the same way as it was on boilers. He retired from day-to-day activities at the yard in 1861, the year before the yard's most famous (infamous?) ship, the *Alabama*, had been completed in secrecy for the American Confederacy.

Sentiments on Merseyside, certainly among the rich, were for the South in the American Civil War because the cotton industry was so important to Liverpool's prosperity. Poor people, often themselves working in dreadful conditions for low pay, had sympathy for the plantation slaves, as had some influential "liberal" families. There was, however, understandable pride in the exploits of the *Alabama*. The wives of merchants particularly ignored the question of slavery, seeing the Confederates as romantic rebels, fighting for the freedom and autonomy of their states in a loosely federated nation. Much was raised for their cause on Merseyside. The *Alabama*, 1,050 tons, screw-steam sloop-of-war, was at sea for 534 of her 657 days. In that time, she captured or burned 65 Union merchant ships, but was sunk off the coast of Cherbourg, France, on June 11, 1864, by the sloop-of-war, the USS *Kearsarge*. After the war an arbitration court in Geneva judged that Britain should pay the American government £3.25m in compensation for the losses sustained.

Laird married Elizabeth Hurry and they had three sons, William, John and Henry, all of whom followed their father into the yard. Laird himself became Birkenhead's first mayor and served as the borough's conservative MP between 1861 and 1874. After his death, caused by a riding accident, a statue was commissioned from Albert Bruce-Joy. It was unveiled in Hamilton Square in 1877, but was moved a short distance to make room for the war memorial in front of the town hall. Laird is buried in the graveyard at Birkenhead Priory.

JOSEPH PAXTON (1803–1865) was the seventh son born into a farming family in Milton Bryan, Bedfordshire. Paxton began his career as a boy gardener and after a number of jobs took up a position at the Horticultural Society's Chiswick Gardens. There, he met William Cavendish, the sixth

Duke of Devonshire, who appointed the impressive 20-year-old head gardener at Chatsworth House, near Bakewell, Derbyshire.

There, he advanced his ideas for landscape gardening, while building a 300ft conservatory, planting an arboretum, and laying out a model village. This work led to him designing his masterpiece, the Crystal Palace for the Great Exhibition of 1851. Queen Victoria knighted Paxton for this service to his country.

In 1842, Paxton and James Pennethorne had designed Princes Park, Liverpool. Fifty acres of a site owned by Richard Vaughan Yates was developed as a park. Significantly, most of it was open to the public. A further 40-acres were developed for housing, which helped finance the project. Later in the decade this idea was developed on a grander scale over the 226-acres of Birkenhead Park, where the sale of houses also helped finance the project, which became the world's first fully public park. Wirral Borough Council now runs it. Liverpool City Council runs Princes Park. In common with many great Victorians, Paxton believed passionately in the betterment of conditions for the underprivileged and he served as the Liberal MP for Coventry from 1854 until his death.

CHARLES CAMMELL (1803–1879) was a Sheffield steel maker. In 1903, the company that he founded joined with the shipyard begun in Birkenhead by William Laird, to form Cammell Laird Shipbuilders.

OLIVIERI FAMILY. Sisters Julie and Mary Peronia came from Viareggio, Italy. Julie married Olivo Olivieri and Mary married Freddie Fabri. Italians had been settling in Merseyside for generations. In the earlier part of the nineteenth century their numbers included musicians, doctors, engineers, and skilled craftsmen, particularly terrazzo and mosaic layers, who had melted into the middle-classes. But poorer Italians followed in the late 1800s. These were tough, resolute and deeply religious people. Many stayed in an area off Liverpool's Scotland Road, known locally as Little Italy. They mixed easily with Irish people who had already settled there, establishing a strong Roman Catholic Community, served by numerous parish churches. These Italians followed the trades, which have made them famous in cities across the western world – catering, ice cream scooping, frying fish, tailoring, boxing, singing and organ-grinding.

Julie, Mary, Olivo and Freddie came to Britain in the 1920s, but instead of Liverpool, the Fabris started catering in Birkenhead, while the Olivieris went to Dundee. But the families kept in touch. After the war, the Olivieris, who had four children, Dennis, Ronnie, Olga and Yolando, opened their famous café and ice cream stall in Birkenhead. Located opposite Hamilton Square railway station, it became a favoured meeting place for people from both sides of the river. Sadly, it disappeared as part of urban regeneration.

DOMINIC (DOM) VOLANTE (1905–1972) was one of the most famous sons of Liverpool's Little Italy.

Dom was one of 14 children born to the organ-grinder Vincenzo Volante and his wife, Marie, both originally from Naples. Money was very short but the Volantes were cultured people, as were many of their neighbours, who benefited from an education in the local Catholic schools. Vincenzo could speak several languages and occasionally earned fees as an interpreter in the burgeoning port. The family's earnings enabled them to have a plumbed bath in the house, an almost unknown luxury in the neighbourhood.

Dom attended Holy Cross School, near the family's home in Gerard Street, off Scotland Road. It was there as an eight-year-old that he had his first fight. It was against a bigger boy, who wanted the tin can that Dom had been using as a football. In time-honoured fashion, other children formed a circle around them, as the boys wrestled, kicked and punched on the knee-skinning concrete. Dom won. A few streets away, his good father turned the handle on his barrel organ and its melody wheezed into the foggy air.

© DEBRA D'ANNUNZIO

In those days, the approaches to an official boxing ring were known as "Mugs' Alleys". Untested boxers and broken pugs would hang around in their shorts and vests, hoping that someone billed to appear would pull out, leaving the other man with nobody to fight. The organisers would then look for a likely substitute, prepared to take a battering to put some potatoes on the table or to buy his sweetheart a pretty frock. Under the cigar smoke, you could see, the agents in their fancy suits, alongside the fast-talking bookies and the reporters in their pork pie hats.

But Dom had a keen mind, as well as fists as fast as two wasps in a jar. At the age of 12 he began his own club on Gerard Street. It was tuppence to join. The boys put on exhibition bouts, charging people a penny to watch. A few years later, "Pa" Taylor, a boxing promoter at the famous Liverpool Stadium, offered Dom professional terms. Between 1921 and 1936, the organ-grinder's son had 130 fights, winning 94 (55 by knock-outs). He lost 25 and drew 11. Dom was a southpaw, who relied on toughness and technique rather than style. At the time, Nel Tarleton (1906–1956) was another fine Liverpool boxer, possessed of dancing feet and deft swerves. The two men were firm friends but, inevitably, they had to fight each other. Tarleton won three of their four bouts. This didn't in any way diminish their friendship and they ran a sideline as entertainers. Dom played the mouth organ while Nel danced.

Despite never being a champion, Dom had a high reputation and he would fight many of the best featherweight boxers in Europe and the USA, which he toured in 1930, winning four and drawing five of his bouts. The drawn match was against Harry Carlton. More than 18,000 people at Madison Square Gardens watched it. The New York reporters declared that it had been the most exciting fight in boxing history.

After his retirement from the ring, Dom became a fitness trainer and a boxing instructor on Cunard's luxury liners, including the *Mauretania*, the *Queen Mary* and the *Queen Elizabeth*. In this capacity, he helped keep trim such stars as Bette Davis, Nancy Sinatra and Joseph Cotton. In the late 1950s, he was on board the Britannic when he gave some instructions to a young steward called John Prescott, a broad-shouldered fellow with a certain swagger. He didn't know then that Prescott's future lay in politics, not catering or boxing.

In the 2001 General Election, Prescott was campaigning in Rhyl, North Wales. A farm worker called Craig Evans joined the crowd, many of whom were protesting about the Government's policies on agriculture. Evans threw an egg that struck the former waiter's round head and burst. Prescott retaliated with a punch, perhaps guided by Dom's ghost, which landed sweetly on the protestor's jaw. Although Prescott's contribution to the governance of Britain will soon be forgotten, his place in history was secured by that punch.

A plaque to Dom's memory and trophy in his name were presented to the Salisbury Amateur Boxing Club, Liverpool, in 2009. Debra D'Annunzio, who wrote a book about Liverpool's Italian families in 2008, presented both.

TONY BROWN, ARTIST (1961–). It is appropriate that this Great Liverpudlian should have been born at the dawn of Merseybeat; his infant mewling joining the distant throb of drums and the wailing guitars in a city, where the young musicians had switched from skiffle to rock and roll to give the world a new style of popular music. Tony is a fine guitarist himself, whose admiration for The Beatles is unreserved.

But it is for his painting that he is now renowned. As we approached 2007, the city's elders and leaders and the new breed of thrusting PRs and marketing men and women were conscious that something should be done to celebrate the 800th anniversary of King John granting Liverpool the Royal Charter (Letters Patent), which gave high blessing to the development of the port.

This year was the ideal prelude to 2008, when Liverpool was to be the European Capital of Culture. The meetings were in full hum, the coffee was percolating, the clipboards were being brandished, chalk squeaked on the blackboards; men and women rolled up their sleeves and the Belgian biscuits were served. But Tony was working on his idea for 100 portraits of Liverpudlians, who had meant a lot to him.

Most of these people were close friends of his or members of his family, but a few were famous. Among the famous were The Beatles, the writers, Alan Bleasdale and Jimmy McGovern, and the actors, Dean Sullivan, Pauline Daniels and Andrew Schofield. To the background of the portraits, Tony added small pictures, photographs and words, which left the viewer with a biographical impression of the person. Also, attached to each display easel were the details of the subjects' lives and beliefs.

For months Tony worked on this project, closing himself away from the rest of the world. Up to that point, he had been most successful with his conventional portraits of the famous and his exquisite "doodle" drawings of people and places, such as the waterfronts at Liverpool and New York – just a few brilliantly executed lines seemed to form a complete picture. This work gained him important commissions. Bloomingdale's, the New York department store, was among those to sell items carrying his pictures, as the two cities worked together to promote their roles in The Beatles' story. His drawings are now featured on T-shirts, plates, towels, running shoes and posters.

But his portraits were to make an even greater mark in popular culture. He called the exhibition 100 Heads Thinking As One. It became the highlight of 2007, moving seamlessly into the European culture year.

The exhibition has been shown at the Anglican Cathedral, The Catholic Cathedral, St George's Hall and the Williamson Art Gallery in Birkenhead, as well as numerous schools, shops and public halls.

Praise was heaped on Tony. "A project carved out of the soul of Liverpool," said Alastair Machray, editor of the *Liverpool Echo*, and Sara Wilde, managing director of Trinity Mirror North West and North Wales, declared that Tony was "a genius".

"I derive a lot of my inspiration from keeping one foot in the past, one in the present and walking a bridge for my love of the traditional and an urge to constantly experiment," said Tony himself. "The process lies in the need to produce a fully rounded portrait of the sitter – his/her life and all its special things. It is an opportunity to share in their memories, thoughts, wishes, dreams and ambitions. In late 2004, I became inspired to say something with my work and thought that 100 portraits would be a worthy tribute to the city. It was a sense of roots, thanks, acknowledgement and respect. Then I thought of bereavement and loss and devoted my energies towards a monument to our city's finest asset, its people. I didn't want to start off with

a shopping list of heads. It wasn't a chore, though it was incredibly hard work. We met laughed and talked a lot with the heads."

Although Tony has had some artistic training, his techniques are largely self-taught. He feels his passion for Liverpool comes from the Celtic background that he shares with so many Liverpudlians. In his case, it is a quixotic balance of Scottish and Irish blood.

But there is always that moment, isn't there, always that telling moment. Could it have been when Tony saw his father, John Brown, a fine commercial artist, climbing a ladder with a sweeping brush to paint a giant Father Christmas on the wall outside a shop in London Road, Liverpool? This was being done for an episode of *Z Cars* (the BBC police series set on Merseyside. Its theme tune is an adaptation of the folk song, Johnny Todd, and Everton fans adopted it as their own).

Well, you can see the delicate brushstrokes hanging on the walls in the grand galleries. But Father Christmas on a shop wall was painting for the people.

Tony's ancestors settled in the Scotland Road area of Liverpool, but his family moved to Birkenhead when he was 10.

"Determination is a great Liverpool quality, you could call it old-fashioned gumption," said Tony. "There are almost equal doses of eternal positivity and eternal negativity in every Liverpool person. They have a stand-alone spirit. Every person standing on either bank of this river has a spirit unlike any other, a wandering soul. Overall we are less English and more Celtic. Most creative thought from Liverpool is from a Celtic scene.

"Of course, this didn't mean much to careers' teachers, but it did to my parents. My late mother, Margaret (Brennan), was a rock and so was my dad. My mother was naturally very intelligent and academic. She couldn't go to university because she was the eldest in a big family that couldn't afford it. But she should have been a professor.

"I had this magic feeling about the 100 portraits. I still have. Not matter what I do and I do want to say something else, it will be the best thing I have ever done. I will never do anything on that scale again. It took a lot out of me and my wife, Lorraine, who has supported me through thick and thin."

Tony feels that The Beatles remain the great influence on modern Liverpool. "Most people could think of their names easily, but they couldn't name the last four popes," he said. "It is not solely because they came from Liverpool, but when you are young you look for the voice and you see TV, which is a blinkered version of culture. There was the BBC voice and the clipped accent. You didn't see anyone who looked like you and you didn't hear anyone who sounded like you until The Beatles came along. They made me immensely proud to have come from where I come from and for my parents to have come from where they came from. I like to live in the past because it reminds me of where I come from and where I am going."

This mingling of the past, the present and the future into a single continuous time is a quality common to many Great Liverpudlians.

GEORGE HARRISON (1943–2001) was a writer, wit, film producer, peace campaigner and seeker after spiritual explanations. He achieved international recognition as the lead guitarist with The Beatles, the most successful group in the history of popular music.

Harrison's death had been expected. It did not, therefore, excite quite the same level of international mourning as Lennon's had. But the sorrow was deep and it matured into an understanding of just how important George had been to the group. His early image as the "quiet Beatle" seemed absurd in the light of all his achievements, not only as fine musician and songwriter, but also as a man who wanted to make a contribution to life.

Taxman is probably the most satirical of all The Beatles' songs, carrying the brilliant line, "my advice to those who die, declare the pennies on your eyes". When talking about The Beatles now, I am struck by how many people say, "He was always my favourite". This is particularly true of the women who had grown up with him. At first the reason for this was not obvious. After all Lennon and McCartney had always been presented as the most talented, but then I saw the reason. With his high cheekbones, slow smile and steady stare, George had been the best looking. In the modern sense of the word he was the "cool" Beatle. Also, he seemed most aware that the there was something slightly wrong in a world, which could give four young men from Liverpool so much fame and adoration for singing songs.

He was, indeed, a philosopher. His pursuit of truth, through Eastern religion and other routes, was not dotty, as it had been portrayed in the media, but an expression of his bewilderment about the world around us. He was perhaps at his happiest as a member of another group, the Traveling Wilburys (Harrison, Jeff Lynne, Tom Petty, Roy Orbison and Bob Dylan), which was admired for its good-fun music, but not worshipped, in the mad way The

Beatles had been. Their first album in 1988 was generally acclaimed and the follow-up two years later also did well. The obvious friendship between the players in their various Wilbury guises shines through.

Of course, co-operation between friends had been a strength of Harrison's. In 1971, he linked up with Ravi Shankar, the Indian sitar player, to organise the two concerts performed before 40,000 people at Madison Square Gardens, New York, for Bangladesh, a country which had been devastated by war and famine. His status in the rock world helped Harrison attract such stars as Dylan, Eric Clapton, Billy Preston and Leon Russell.

Eight years later, Harrison and his business partner, Denis O'Brien, came to their rescue of his friends in the Monty Python team of comic actors and writers (Graham Chapman, John Cleese, Eric Idle, Terry Gilliam, Terry Jones and Michael Palin) and writers, who were struggling to finance their film, *Monty Python's Life of Brian*. Harrison and O'Brien formed HandMade Films to save the project. During his involvement with the company, which lasted until 1994, HandMade produced such classic films as *The Long Good Friday*, *Time Bandits*, *Mona Lisa*, *Withnail and I*, and *The Lonely Passion of Judith Hearne*. There were also some clunkers.

Candles still glow for George of The Beatles.

JOHN LENNON (1940–1980) was an artist, writer, rebel, philosopher and peace-campaigner. That may seem like a description of almost any educated Liverpudlian, who had grown up in the post-war years, but he was also a guitarist and harmonica player with The Beatles, the most successful group in the history of popular music. With his song-writing partner, Paul McCartney, Lennon was responsible for some of the finest songs of the twentieth century. Although they are released under their joint names, many of the later ones were in fact solo compositions.

David Webster's statue of John Lennnon on Mathew Street

Lennon's death on December 8, 1980, after being shot near his home in New York by a crazed fan, who otherwise would have been of no consequence at all, provoked international mourning. It could be argued that Lennon's political importance and influence on the peace movement has been exaggerated, but his contribution to popular culture is immeasurable.

His statue by Tom Murphy stands in the Liverpool John Lennon Airport. Murphy chose the pose of the thinking rebel with strutting legs, but blinking eyes. That is the Lennon people will remember, rather than the smiling "Mop Top" created to promote The Beatles in the early days of their success.

There is much of Liverpool in Lennon and of Lennon in Liverpool. He was the kind man with a cruel streak, the intellectual who didn't bloom until he escaped the confines of Quarry Bank School; the peace campaigner, who had been quite violent in his youth; the hard rocker, who wrote sensitive songs of yearning and loss; the cynic, who was also a sentimentalist, a very strong characteristic among Liverpudlians.

PAUL MCCARTNEY (1942–) is the multi-instrumentalist, writer and artist, who rose to international celebrity as the bass guitarist with The Beatles. With his song-writing partner, John Lennon, he was responsible for some of the finest songs of the twentieth century. Although they were released under joint names, many of the later ones were in fact solo compositions.

Paul is sensitive to the criticism that he was in some ways the softer partner, with the more conventional, suburban outlook. Both Beatles were from the suburbs and attendance at grammar school (Liverpool Institute in the case of McCartney) gave them a sound basic education, even if it wasn't entirely appreciated. The contrasts in their styles can be seen most strongly in Lennon's *Strawberry Fields Forever* and McCartney's *Penny Lane*, both songs remembering their childhood in Liverpool. At the time of their release in 1967, the psychedelic mood of Lennon's song appealed more to the critics, who had come to see The Beatles as the spearhead of the "alternative society". Maybe, though, time favours the more directly descriptive *Penny Lane*. McCartney was as eager as any of The Beatles eager to experiment with art and poetry. He greatly admired some surrealistic art, though he quickly differentiated between the good and the pretentious in the work of others.

His songs, though not of the highest lyrical standard, have splendidly memorable melodies. If he had only written *Yesterday*, his reputation would have been secure. It is true that his forays into light-classical composition, painting and poetry have not always been acclaimed, but does a Beatle have to worry about that?

If there had been no Beatles, it is easier to imagine him, rather than the others, doing well as a solo pop singer or composer in the Tin Pan Alley tradition. McCartney has never dismissed his native city and his public returns are always welcomed with great enthusiasm. Liverpool's love of him is reciprocated. It is a tragedy that sections of the vulgar press regarded his love life as more interesting than his songs.

Millions of mums and grandmothers across the world still have pictures of the young Paul clasped in their lockets. His reputation is secure for generations to come – perhaps forever.

RINGO STARR (born 1940 as Richard Starkey) is a musician and natural comedian noted for his lugubrious delivery. There were four Beatles and he was one of them. It is easy to forget that when comparing his contributions to those of the other three.

These days, when The Beatles are being discussed, you often hear critics mentioning his name, almost as an afterthought. This has made the quality of his drumming a subject of much heated debate, heightened by the cruel remark, attributed to Lennon – "Ringo, the best drummer in the world? He's not even the best drummer in The Beatles."

In this harsh spirit, people will conclude that his contribution to the group was marginal. They would have made it without him, they say. Maybe that is so. I am not expert enough to offer an opinion on his drumming, but I do know that most Merseybeat aficionados believe that he was a very fine drummer, perfectly suited to the style of The Beatles. And if you look at early pictures of the "Fab Four" it is hard to imagine them without him. His face belongs. Moreover, in those days it was widely assumed that the rebels of rock music would quickly change into all-round family entertainers and that would be his moment. With his big conk and sad smile, Ringo looked like a man, who could appear in panto or on a variety act at the end-of-the-pier.

American families took to him during the heady years in the mid 1960s when The Beatles were at their peak. He could have been a clown in a silent movie. He was also the most accessible Beatle – funny in an open way. John wouldn't have liked to have a custard pie pushed into his face, but Ringo – well, he was a good-natured sort of chap. There seemed to be something distant and mysterious about the other three and this made them slightly threatening. They shook their heads in the choruses of chirpy songs, but there were also thinkers and that was dangerous. There were too many thinkers in the world. Additionally, it was argued that Ringo was the best natural actor in the group with a hint of Charlie Chaplin in his demeanour. People can judge that for themselves by watching again The Beatles' films *A Hard Day's Night* (1964) and *Help!* (1965).

Anyway, Ringo did very well out of being a Beatle and on January 11, 2008, he appeared on the roof of St George's Hall, Liverpool, before an estimated 25,000 people to open the city's celebrations as the European Capital of Culture. The following day, he performed at the city's Echo Arena. It is generally accepted that these were not moments of the highest triumph in his long career.

After The Beatles, Ringo had continued performing as a singer and a drummer, raising two fingers in the peace salute to large crowds, as a gesture of faith in the ideals he had promoted with the other three Beatles. He was possibly best known as the narrator of the TV stories about *Thomas the Tank Engine* (1984–1990). But it is on hearing the deep, slow magnificence of his Liverpool voice that you can see him – the Beatle with sad eyes. He was the drummer in the greatest group in the world. Whenever you say "John, Paul, George," someone will add, "and Ringo". He was a Beatle.

BRIAN EPSTEIN (1934–1967) was the manager of The Beatles. He died in what has become known to popular history as "the year of love". It was the long summer of Old Testament hairstyles, beads, Eastern wisdom in cigarette card form, the scent of marijuana smoke, and a tendency for middle-class boys to address everyone as "man".

Pixies and elves cavorted in the dreams of a generation, which was ostensibly seeking an alternative way. In truth, many dressed up at the weekends, but returned to their desks on Monday, a little groggy, but still calling the boss "sir", rather than "man". The Beatles were right at the heart of all this. So Epstein had a problem. As a manager he was completely devoted to his "boys". He had been a wonderful manager for them.

You have to remember that before him most managers had treated their pop stars as commodities with a very limited shelf-life. This meant that you had to sell as much of them as possible, before their appeal faded and they were cast out to the Land of Nostalgia, pantos and summer shows. Epstein's relationship to The Beatles was different. They were his friends and he admired them greatly. Some writers have said that he fancied them, particularly John. There can be little doubt that a homosexual man, who had endured unhappy spells in boarding schools and the Army, would have found them attractive. Indeed, that might have helped him to appreciate their appeal to girls.

Although The Beatles and Epstein had much in common, there were also crucial differences. It is true that they would often have drawn similar conclusions from the their amusing observations of life, but Epstein was at least nominally in charge. However, the balance of this power was deeply compromised by his devotion to them. There was no question of Lennon seeing Epstein as "the guv", except, perhaps, ironically. Also, he was a Jew and they were Gentiles in an age when anti-Semitic jokes and sentiments were expressed on buses and in pubs, cafés, offices and factories in a casual manner, never heard by the sensitive ears of those raised on the politically correct values of the present time. Of course, that didn't mean that any of The Beatles were racists – far from it. They were tolerant of differences to an extent that would have been surprising to many in the early 1960s. Even so, they would have absorbed some of the feelings then prevalent. More significantly, he was the businessman and they were the artists. He controlled the purse strings and they had the talent.

One of the many contradictions in Britain is that business acumen is accepted, but not generally praised. The businessman does not stand with the sportsmen and women, the musicians and the poets, the actors and the designers. He is accepted but not admired by the general public. Businessmen might receive gongs, but these are usually for their charitable work done in conjunction with commercial success. This is extraordinary in a country that built an immense trading empire and developed institutions in the City of London, which influenced the world's finances. But it is true.

Epstein died of an accidental drugs' overdose on August 2, 1967. At the time The Beatles and an entourage of instant gurus were in Bangor, North Wales, listening to the squeaky prattlings of the Maharishi Mahesh Yogi, who was, apparently, not above squeezing a nicely rounded bottom on his quest for the truth. It was understood that Epstein would have joined them after the Bank Holiday weekend. But he died before that was possible.

At the time, I was on a camping holiday with some friends in Abersoch, North Wales. We are all very much taken up with the mood of the time and spoke with affected hippie voices, "man". I tried to visualise Epstein, with his smart suits and short hair, slipping into a kaftan bedecked with petals. It is to be sure an uneasy picture.

The immediate question was (and still is) – would The Beatles have made in without him? I think the answer is "yes, to an extent", but they would not have developed into the composers of such brilliant music. Epstein's genius lay in allowing them the time and the space to do that. There has been criticism of his deals in the USA, his failure to realise the full potential of The Beatles as a merchandising brand, but didn't he have higher ambition for his boys than to be forever smiling Mop Tops on tea towels? Epstein had other Top Ten stars on his books, but The Beatles were special. He knew that. The world should be grateful to him for enabling four young men to make music, their music.

An excellent portrait of him by Tony Brown was commissioned by the Neptune Theatre, Liverpool, in 1999.

WILFRED OWEN (1893–1918) was a gentle man, a romantic lover of flowers and country churches and simple suburban values, who became a great poet after seeing and feeling and touching the suffering of the other young men that he met in the trenches of the Great War.

They had all been denied the fumblings and the midnight kisses, the birthdays, the hymns, and the squeezed hands of home, for something so terrible that he felt, deep within himself, that it was his duty to tell us about it.

"My subject is war and the pity of war. The poetry is in the pity," he wrote of his purpose.

And so Wilfred Owen became the finest war poet in our language, writing from his own experiences as a soldier. In *Anthem for Doomed Youth* he told of how everything was different for the soldiers, plucked from the factories, the shops and colleges of England – "What passing-bells for those who die as cattle? Only the monstrous anger of the guns. Only the stuttering Rifles' rapid rattle can patter our their hasty orisons ..."

If it had not been for that war, Owen would have been a minor poet at best, writing pretty sonnets for forgotten magazines, while earning his living as the teacher of bored pupils. Fate is strange and terrible.

He was born to Tom and Susan Owen, who had a large, brick house on the outskirts of Oswestry. In the past, Socialists have tried to bag him as one of their own – the proletarian poet from poor stock, but that was not the case. Wilfred was a middle-class boy. Susan's father, Alderman Edward Shaw, was a fomer mayor of the town. On her side, the family were well-to-do. Unhappily, however, Susans's brother, Edward, had squandered much of their money on drink and gambling. In 1897, they had to sell the house and the following year Susan, Tom and their three children moved to Birkenhead, where he had been appointed stationmaster at Woodside railway station. This was not a lowly position. Very few people had cars then and the railways were of the utmost importance. Wilfred was enrolled at Birkenhead Insitute, a school of high aspirations, which served the sons of merchants and the emerging professional class. It provided a sound basic education. While he was attending his classes there, the family lived in houses in Willmer Road, Elm Grove and Milton Street. They seemed to have been a pious, evangelical family and Wilfred attended Bible lessons at Christ Church in Birkenhead's prosperous suburb of Oxton. The family were in Birkenhead for nearly four years, before Tom Owen moved to Shrewsbury to take up another senior appointment with the railways.

After leaving school in Shrewsbury, Wilfred worked for a while as the assistant to a clergyman in Dunsden, near Reading. He had passed the matriculation exam into the University of London, but not with sufficiently high grades for a scholarship. So he decided to work. In 1913, he settled in Bordeaux to teach English at the Berlitz School of Languages. He then took up a post as a private tutor to a rich family in the Pyrenees.

On October 21, 1915, he enlisted with the Artists' Rifles and began training in England. In June the following year, he was commissioned as a second lieutenant into the Manchester Regiment. By 1917, following dreadful experiences of death and suffering in the trenches, he was sent to the Craiglockhart War Hospital, near Edinburgh, to be treated for neurasthenia (shellshock). There, he met the older poet Siegfried Sassoon, who immediately spotted the potential in Owen's work. He advised the young man on some matters of style, though never substance. Owen returned to the Western Front a transformed being. From then until his death, his bravery and dedication was unbridled. Again, interested parties have tried to bag him as one of their own, but there is no evidence from his poems, such as *Anthem for Doomed Youth*, *Spring Offensive*, *Strange Meeting* and *Greater Love*, that Owen was a pacifist. He certainly mourned for the victims of war, but he was a soldier and a very good one, who wanted to tell us, in language of bitter beauty, how it had been for him and his comrades. In 1918, he was awarded the Military Cross. The citation read: "For conspicuous gallantry and devotion to duty in the attack on the Fonsomme Line on October 12. On their company commander becoming a casualty, he assumed command and showed fine leadership and resisted a heavy counter-attack. He personally manipulated a capture of an enemy machine-gun from an isolated position and inflicted considerable losses on the enemy. Throughout, he behaved most gallantly."

As the church bells pealed peace on Armistice Day, November 11, 1918, a telegram was delivered to his family's semi-detached home in Shrewsbury. Wilfred had been killed shepherding his men across the Sambre Canal near the little French town of Ors. He is buried in the cemetery there – the corner of a foreign field, as his fellow poet Rupert Brooke had written at the beginning of the war.

In 1962, Owen's poems were included in Benjamin Britten's *War Requiem*.

THE SEARCHERS (classic line-up John McNally, guitar and vocals, born 1941; Mike Pender, guitar and vocals, born 1942; Chris Curtis, drummer and vocals, 1941–2005; Tony Jackson, bass and vocals, 1938–2003). There were numerous changes in personnel before and after their most successful period in the mid 1960s. For example, Frank Allen (born 1943) replaced Jackson in 1964 and has been with the group ever since.

In common with most Mersey groups, The Searchers began as skifflers, taking their name from the 1956 western directed by John Ford and starring John Wayne. In other ways, too, they followed the usual path, performing in Hamburg as well as local venues. Although they lacked the songwriting talent of Lennon and McCartney, The Searchers at least matched The Beatles as musicians and singers. Their early record sales were sensational in Britain and quite strong in the USA. In Britain, *Sweets for My Sweet*, *Needles and Pins* and *Don't Throw Your Love Away* were all number ones. *Sugar and Spice*, *When You Walk in the Room* and *Goodbye My Love* were major hits. Their decision to record Malvina Reynolds' *What Have they Done to the Rain?*, with its obvious reference to nuclear war, suggested that The Searchers were influenced by the increasing association between rock/pop music and politics. It reached 13 in the British chart, but they failed to follow this lead and develop a reputation as hip thinkers in the style of some of their competitors. So record sales fell off, though the group was still touching the bottom reaches of the charts in the early 1970s.

For a while, they had kept up with The Beatles, Rolling Stones, the Kinks and The Who, but the absence of a major songwriting talent was to cost them dearly. In popular culture The Searchers had done something else for Liverpool, in reminding people that the Cavern was not the only important club in the development of Merseybeat. Just up the road at 13 Temple Street stood the Iron Door. In those crazy days, beatniks and young artists and poets, such as Roger McGough, Brian Patten and Adrian Henri, stalked the parish and slunk around the cellar dives, like prophets in jeans. It was quite a time in the city and its young bohemians, who were much influenced by the Beat writers of America – Gregory Corso, Allen Ginsberg, Jack Kerouac and others. Many gathered behind the towering bricks of this old warehouse called the Iron Door. There you could hear Priscilla White singing *Fever* with rare intensity and some respect for the melody, while blond Fred Fowell had his hair dyed black to add authenticity to his Elvis impressions. Sometimes they would be joined by John Lennon and his friend Stu Sutcliffe, a very fine and sensitive artist, who usually wore a floppy cowboy hat. John and Stu are both dead. Miss White (first heard by Brian Epstein at the Iron Door) became Cilla Black and Mr Fowell is Freddie Starr, the comedian.

The Iron Door closed in the 1970s and in that grand tradition was demolished to make room for a car park. Nearly all the major jazz acts played there, including Kenny Ball, Ronnie Scott, Tubby Hayes and Johnny Dankworth. They preferred its plusher surrounds to the starker Cavern, where the stench from the lavatory drains was a particular torment to those with sensitive nostrils. Perversely, the Iron Door was also preferred by the hip set, who would make peculiar arrangements for kipping the night there. Poems, or "pomes", as the local pronunciation had it, about the bomb's mushroom cloud and lost love arose from the dimpled cushions and dank sleeping bags of the Iron Door. It was not unknown for the imaginations of these poets, waiting for publishers, to be stimulated (or deadened?) by illegal substances. The Iron Door had opened in 1960 and, like the Cavern, started as a jazz club, which tolerated beat groups and performers such as The Undertakers, Gerry and the Pacemakers, Beryl Marsden, The Mojos, The Remo Four, The Big Three and Rory Storm and the Wild Ones. Although The Beatles were associated with the Cavern, they did perform at the Iron Door seven times, while The Searchers made occasional visits to the Cavern. Another regular at "the Door" was Brendan McCormack and his group Rikki and the Redstreaks. Lennon reportedly thought Brendan was the best guitarist in Liverpool. He was also a very fine classical guitarist, whose death in 2009 was much mourned.

THE MERSEY SOUND POETS (ROGER MCGOUGH, BRIAN PATTEN AND ADRIAN HENRI).

The possibilities of language are stretched and explored in Liverpool. We love words. Some people attribute this to all that Irish blood flowing in the Mersey. They could be right. Travel to the Birkenhead banks of the river and listen to the weary Tranmere Rovers' fan describing one of his team's defenders, who is lacking in the necessary pace. The poor chap shakes his old head in despair. "I have seen milk turn faster than that lad," he mutters to himself.

A man in obviously low spirits enters a pub. "He looks as happy as a pacifist at a weapons' convention," observes the unpublished poet at the bar. The fellow of obvious gay leanings is described is "as queer as a nine bob note" – a reference, which might mystify those only familiar with modern money.

The humorous use of words is the revenge of the man, who feels that is talents have been overlooked by conventional society. On Merseyside – perhaps in Britain as a whole – we are accustomed to the brightest people being at the bottom of the pile and the dimmest at the top. To many of us, rulers and bosses are not despised or hated. Instead, they are recognised for what they really are – figures of fun. With power comes absurdity.

During the 1960s, mockery and satire were very much in vogue. As we entered a period of plenty after the tight, grey years of rationing, which followed the war, the pavements were strode by a new elite – confident but often disrespectful of the tired old ways. These were the boys and girls, who had emerged from the grammar schools with "the Latin", like their public school contemporaries, but they had also been hardened on the streets and in the new high-rise flats. They had visited the university of life as well as the groves of academe. In Liverpool they were represented by pop singers, writers, comedians and a new generation of poets, who did not take their inspiration from daffodils or gurgling brooks. With the passing of time these rebels would be absorbed into mainstream society, in the traditional British way. But for a while they were strong, taking as their themes the fear of nuclear destruction, race and class prejudice; and the vulgarity and excess of commercialism, then familiar to all through TV advertising. In the past people had been angry about such things, but these people were clever, keeping their cool, while lampooning authority. They had all been taught the poems of Shakespeare, Tennyson, Wordsworth, Coleridge, the Brontë sisters and so on, but they wanted to write new poems about now. Not only that, they wanted to perform them before "live" audiences, as opposed to "dead" ones, perhaps.

Younger readers might not immediately appreciate just how revolutionary that idea was. The works of great British poets had to a large extent been ruined by generations of teachers, who had insisted on their pupils learning them line for line, so that they could be recited in the meaningless sing-song tones of the classroom, with a rap on the knuckles being the reward for a forgotten word. Poems were learned for exams and then forgotten. Even now, you can see old-timers twisting themselves into agonised poses, as they try to recall the second line of a poem. It was always the second line. Nearly everyone could remember the first line and then it would be tumpty-tumpty-tumpty-tum as they advanced on the rhyming word. There were, however, exceptions to all this. Among the exceptions were American poets – those Beats, who had taken their name from "beatification", and our own Dylan Thomas from Swansea, who had died from alcoholism soon after completing *Under Milk Wood*, his play for voices. They had read their works to an adoring public.

In Liverpool, poets began gathering in sympathetic pubs and cellars to read their offerings, though it was the Everyman Theatre that would make a few of them famous. McGough, Patten and Henri were at the core of this movement.

ROGER MCGOUGH (1937–).

With his nobly domed head and the sparkling, owl-like glasses of an agony aunt, McGough may fit easily enough into Guardianesque England, as one of the ablest contributors to those chattering classes, who sip red wine from Chile while picking slivers of blue-veined cheese from teeth carefully preserved by private dentists. But he is a truly working-class man, even if he doesn't reveal his memories of a lavvy in the backyard at the drop of an olive from its stick.

But those memories are there. For this punster poet of rare genius had many times felt the vicious strap of Christian Brothers across the hand that could spin a cricket ball like a demon at the coal shovel, which served as the wickets down the backyard square, where the lavatory butted into the boundary. This was the imaginative and sensitive Roger playing for Lancashire in his freshly pressed white flannels, while dreaming of triumphs at his terraced home in Ruthven Road, Seaforth, about four miles from Liverpool.

Working-class then didn't mean uncultured in the way that it would now. The daily papers and the wireless were informative and most people had read good books. The ability to play musical intruments and perform at family gatherings was widespread and would prove an immense asset to young boys and girls joining the skiffle craze. People cooked for themselves and kept fit

through the exercises of daily routine. The idea of stewing in front of the telly and eating instant food, would have seemed totally wrong to the working-class families of Liverpool.

McGough's father, also Roger, was a shy, wise and kindly docker married to Mary. Roger was born to them when Hitler was scratching his bottom and staring at the globe with foaming lust. They were a loving family (the McGoughs not the Hitlers), who made the best of life, despite the efforts of the Luftwaffe to spoil everything. Both parents were thrilled, though perhaps a little anxious a few years later, when their son passed the 11-plus exam, enabling him to move from the Star of the Sea Primary School to St Mary's College, Crosby. There, he did well enough to enter Hull University, where he did a joint honours degree in Geography and French.

Teaching was an obvious choice for a boy from his background and McGough had spells teaching at St Kevin's School, Kirkby, and the Mabel Fletcher College, Liverpool. But the poetry scene, beginning to bloom in harmony with the beat groups, drew him in. In addition to his rhymes and brilliant word-play, McGough was a bit of a dandy. Only after discovering the secrets of girls, had he abandoned his early ambition to be the Pope, whom, he had observed, was always well turned out. So, for a while in the late sixties, he ran a dual career – as one of the three Mersey Sound poets (with Henri and Patten) and as a member of the Scaffold, the satirical sketches and pop group, whose other members were Mike McCartney (brother of Paul, born in 1936, who later became a successful photographer and writer) and John Gorman (born 1936 in Birkenhead, who became a TV entertainer and director and continues to be a brilliant performer). Both careers were hugely successful for McGough.

In 1967, Penguin books included the *Mersey Sound* anthology in its *Modern Poets'* series. The book has never been out of print and sales have topped half a million. Ironically, the poems are recited in sing-song voices by children in classrooms, but with more enjoyment that in the days of McGough's schooling. As the poetry was popular, so were the comic turns, poetry and songs of the Scaffold, who were gaining a reputation quite equal to that of many beat groups. This resulted in a series of hits *Thank U Very Much* (number four, 1967), *Do You Remember* (34, 1968), *Lily the Pink* (one, 1968), *Gin, Gan Goolie* (38, 1969) and *Liverpool Lou* (seven, 1974).

McGough's contribution to British poetry is great and was recognised with a CBE in 2004. His anthologies, such as *Watchwords, After the Merrymaking, Sporting Relations, Summer with Monica* and *Everyday Eclipses*, have all been successful, fulfilling his original ambition to bring poetry to ordinary people.

As a presenter of the Radio 4's programme, *Poetry Please*, he has been able to further that ambition. In common with John Betjeman, Dylan Thomas and his old pal Adrian Henri, McGough reads his poems in an unmistakable voice – starting slowly, before rushing on, in the style of water in a tap, which has suddenly cleared an air-bubble.

BRIAN PATTEN (1946–). The purpose of many careers' advisory officers was to thwart the ambition of the boy or girl sitting on the other side of his desk. Brian Patten wanted to be a writer. The careers' officer had given two full minutes to considering Patten, who was leaving Sefton Park Secondary Modern School.

Well, he had been slow learning to read, so the boy probably wouldn't be able to write much, not in the serious world of lists and duplicate forms, anyway. What would be a suitable alternative to writing?

"Butcher's lad?" suggested the job-finder, a course which Patten surprisingly followed. However, the butcher in question knew someone on the *Bootle Times*. Writing for the paper would suit the young man better than boning hams. In truth, he was only marginally more suited to the grind of local journalism. By then Patten was as thin as a mop-stick, with crazy curly hair, like a Lord Byron of the railway embankments and the gas-works.

Usually cub reporters stomp around the magistrates' courts, town halls and police stations, grubbing for stories. But those in charge of such establishments didn't like long hair. This meant that Patten spent much of his time covering garden fetes and bric-a-brac sales, where neat hair was not seen as essential to the production of a good piece. He also wrote about pop music, which he understood, and during his time there met the emerging poets, Adrian Henri and Roger McGough.

By then, the slow-smiling Patten was also writing promising poems, which he hoped to have published. Like Dylan Thomas before him, who had a brief spell as a cub reporter on the *South Wales Echo*, Patten had learned that there was a big difference between poetry and reporting, though some local newspapers did publish the verses of the small town bards. But that was not for Patten, who parted company with the paper and began travelling in Europe and the Middle East. On his return, he was still writing and Philip Unwin heard him read one of his poems on the radio. Unwin thought that Patten sounded like a young man who understood the changing times. So it was that George Allen and Unwin published his first two solo volumes of poetry, *Little Johnny's Confession* and *Notes to the Hurrying Man*. These were on the book shelves at about the same time as *Mersey Sound*, the compilation of work by Patten, Henri and McGough.

Some saw Patten as the moody one of the three. "A tormented soul," people would say, to one another. There probably was some truth in that. Writing poems, indeed any sort of writing, is a lonely pursuit. The desire for that perfection, which teases and flickers just beyond reach, can shred the nerves, but on the few occasions I have spoken to him, Patten has been cheerful enough, if not a glad-handing back-slapper.

His childhood, spent with his mother Stella in Wavertree Vale, was difficult and often unhappy. There were no books in their terraced house to stimulate the boy, who did later demonstrate faint signs of his emerging talent in school essays. But that was not a time for dreamers. "What did your dad do?" I once asked him. "If you ever see him, ask him," replied Patten, revealing that the revered Liverpool poet had not lost his harsh Scouse wit. Indeed, though supposedly shy and reclusive, Patten is a fine performance poet, travelling the country reading his work, a minstrel of the electronic age.

You find, when ginger-stepping the fringes of celebrity, that the shy star is not such a rare phenomenon. In the limelight they perform, giving the public a bit of themselves; away from it, they think. Many of Patten's poems have been written for children, whom he knows from his own experiences are quite capable of appreciating sullen messages and frightening imagery. But there is a lot of fun and surrealism there, too, as is suggested by such titles *Gargling with Jelly, Juggling with Gerbils* and *Thawing Frozen Frogs.*

In the *Doomed Cyclist*, Patten enters right into the mind of a child: "When Mount Kilimanjaro came into view, he wondered what on Earth to do. He swung up through Egypt and the Nile and cycled over a crocodile … He rode through Russia where the biggest hurdle was navigating the Arctic Circle."

Of course, he has also written volumes of adult poetry – *Vanishing Trick, Storm Damages* and *Armada*. "Patten composes rhapsodies and lamentations to the terrible beauty of love," wrote one admirer.

In conversation with me, Patten said: "I think if you write anarchic poems, they just become accessible to kids. You have got to be on the side of the kids. There are so many rules in their world, some of them necessary rules, but it is nice to break them in poems occasionally, do you know what I mean? The humour comes out more strongly when they are read out. When I was a kid you were threatened with poetry. Now it is the opposite. They say, 'If you are not good, you can't come to the poetry reading', not the other way round."

In that simple statement, Patten spoke of the idea that has filled his being.

ADRIAN HENRI (1932–2000) – a great Liverpudlian, though he was born in Birkenhead and brought up in North Wales, where he attended St Asaph Grammar School.

He was the closest we had to an American Beat poet, even looking rather like his friend Allen Ginsberg, but he was a great deal more than that, being a painter, a loyal friend, a patriot to the city and a journalist, as well as a poet.

We have talked before about the ghostly and immortal quality of

Liverpudlians. Well, Henri's voice still dwells with us. I think particularly here of his poem, *Tonight at Noon*. You start of with his volley of images – the supermarkets advertising threepence on everything, happy children being sent to live in homes, World War One generals selling poppies, leaves falling upwards, art galleries being closed to the over 21s. More and more pictures rise in your mind. And then Henri delivers the line, which brings tears to your eyes: "In forgotten graveyards everywhere, the dead will quietly bury the living and you will tell me you love me. Tonight at Noon."

There was a deep almost fruity quality to his voice, though his phrasing and pauses sounded Liverpudlian. In fact, a generation of enthusiastic but less successful local poets adopted similar tones when reading their agonised efforts to girls at the bus-stop. It helped to keep the birth-rate down.

Henri's childhood in North Wales didn't really separate him from his roots. Liverpool's social and emotional links to North Wales were, in some ways, as close as those it had with Ireland. When the rain drummed on the slate roofs of terraced houses in Birkenhead and Liverpool and you sat dry and warm around the coal fires, you could imagine the coughs and the night-wheezes of the quarrymen from Wales, deep in the mountains, brushing the sky.

Now, when you look down now from the heathered hills, near Llanberis Lake, you can see the distant valleys and their villages with the soprano-singing schoolyards, spinsters' pianos, pebbled-dashed respectability, sturdy shops selling firelighters, travel-weary oranges, clothes pegs, deflating tomatoes, condoms, boot polish and yard brushes; and then there are the biscuit-brown chapels built in the frenzy of a religious revival, which straddled the nineteenth and twentieth centuries. Now the people of a less godly age have converted the chapels into small factories, apartments and cafés. But broad men with thumbs like hammers still swell their woollen jackets, as with priestly devotion, they hunker down to rub errant stones back into the walls, built amid the heather and flaming gorse, to mark the boundaries of ownership, so that the sheep don't get lost.

But when the quarries closed and the other industries of North Wales failed, thousands of these men came to Liverpool and Birkenhead as builders, hoping to find the promised land. Instead, they found docks and small terraced streets.

Even so, thousands of churches, schools and houses on Merseyside were built by Welshmen, who also left us with their accents, which could soar to rare pitches in choirs, but had a guttural note in everyday speech – "tara well".

In return for the builders, Merseyside and Manchester sent the North Wales coast its more prosperous retired people and the weekend caravaners. This seaside strip of the country is not regarded as Welsh Wales, like the mountains, but it was Welsh enough in its own way. Here the young Adrian wrote his first poems. From school he studied fine art at King's College,

Newcastle, developing an interest in abstract expressionism and pop art. In this atmosphere, young men and women started to think of art as a living thing – paintings, poems and songs flowing from the same sources. For example, Ray Davies of the Kinks and John Lennon of The Beatles were both art students in their early musical careers. It was a question of emphasis in each individual. Some secured a reputation in one form, usually music, while others concentrated on poetry, painting or sculpture.

Henri was to find outlets for his enthusiastic talents in music, poetry and painting – making Liverpool, particularly the bohemian and racially mixed Liverpool 8 district, his spiritual home. He soon fell in with other like-minded young men, such and Roger McGough and Brian Patten. Togther, they compiled the poems which were collected together in the *Mersey Sound* book published by Penguin.

"I want to paint pictures worth their weight in money, pictures that tramps can live in, pictures that children would find in their stocking on Christmas morning, pictures that teenage lovers can send each other, I want to paint pictures," he wrote.

As soon as people of a certain age read those lines, they will hear his voice. Perhaps, more than the others, Henri was an admirer of the American Beat writers, whose influence could be felt in every coffee-bar in Liverpool at the time. Dusty copies of Jack Kerouac's *On the Road*, were carried round in much the same way as J.R.R. Tolkien's *Lord of the Rings* would be a generation later.

As the movement developed in Liverpool and The Beatles and others gave it a popular front, Henry formed Liverpool Scene, with the musicians and fellow Beats, Andy Roberts, Mike Evans and Mike Hart, gaining the support of the Radio London DJ John Peel.

Peel (1939–2004) was born John Ravenscroft in Heswall, Wirral. He would become famous on BBC Radio 1 for playing music beyond the popular domain.

In commercial terms, Liverpool Scene was not particularly successful. Their LPs, such as *The Incredible New Music Scene* and *Bread on the Night*, appealed only to devotees, but their live performances were much admired, with the leaping and rotund Henri drawing on huge wells of energy.

Meanwhile, he kept painting and his study of meat on a plate won a prize at the important John Moores Liverpool Exhibition of 1972. Despite his physical health not being as strong as his brave performances suggested, Henri kept on painting, writing poems, pieces for the local press, while teaching at schools and colleges. Heart trouble led to a stroke from which he never fully recovered. Henry was a fine man, much loved by his friends, who marvelled at his profound talent and love of simple pleasures. His presence will always be felt in Liverpool.

FREDDIE STARR (1943–). If you were a young chap with sloping shoulders and a nervous disposition, the approach of this man would persuade you to cross the road.

Freddie looked hard. He was born Fred Fowell in the Old Swan area of Liverpool. He didn't learn much from books or teachers, but he understood life and had no intention of ending up in some deadend clerical job. Instead, he worked on building sites and sharpened his reactions in boxing gyms. But like many Liverpudlians of his generation, young Fowell wanted to be a star (or Starr), adopting his stage name to front such groups as the Midnighters and the Thunderbirds.

Freddie was a good singer, who did a fine Elvis impersonation. He was also a good mover, whose swivelling hips excited the usual reaction from teenage girls, but he also had a vivid imagination and a penchant for surrealistic humour. This side of his act, particularly the impersonations, featured strongly in his performances with another group called the Delmonts, with whom he entertained the British troops in Aden and Cyprus in 1967.

With his reputation growing Starr decided to go solo and achieved his breakthrough when he replaced the sick Dick Emery at a shown in Manchester. He received rave reviews and his career took off. The 1970s was his decade. He appeared at many top venues, including the London Palladium, and became a regular on TV, celebrated for his appearances on *Who Do You Do?*.

Well, after Elvis, he did Hitler best – a magnificent, crazy, and profoundly politically incorrect mockery of the Fuhrer at his foaming best (worst?). But then Hitler himself had little time for the niceties of political correctness. Starr's personal life was often troubled and he slipped from the limelight. However, in March 1986, *The Sun* newspaper carried the headline "Freddie Starr Ate My Hamster". The story was completely untrue, but it revived his career and he has continued touring the country as a star.

GEORGE FORMBY (1904–1961) was the buck-toothed son of a music hall star. Born in Wigan, Formby gave the country a version of northern comedy. In numerous slapstick sketches and films, he played a nervous young man pursuing the girl. Although popular at the time, the low-budget films have not aged well.

On the other hand, his playing of the ukulele-banjo made Formby something of a cult figure admired by such performers as Joe Brown, Lonnie Donegan and George Harrison. In fact, Harrison even performed at George Formby Society events. Formby's songs disguised sexual references in their goofy delivery. Among the most successful were *Auntie Maggie's Remedy*, *Chinese Laundry Blues*, *Leaning on the Lamppost* and *With My Little Stick of Blackpool Rock*.

ALISTAIR TAYLOR (1935–2004) was personal assistant to Brian Epstein at NEMs record store and accompanied him to the Cavern on November 9, 1961, to see The Beatles. As the group progressed under Epstein's management, Taylor became their "Mr Fix It". After Epstein's death in 1961, he was appointed general manager of The Beatles' Apple company and as such appeared in an advertisement seeking talent in the *New Musical Express* and *Rolling Stone* dressed as a one-man band. He left Apple in 1969 and later in his career appeared at Beatles' conventions.

GEORGE MELLY (1926–2007). At a time when Liverpool was associated with working-class footballers, pop musicians and comedians, Melly reminded us that Liverpool also had a vibrant middle-class rooted in the professions, shipping, insurance and other mercantile pursuits.

Their sons and daughters were often as rebellious, and often more outrageous, than their working-class contemporaries. This was peculiarly true of Melly, one of the city's greatest twentieth-century figures. On one occasion, Melly had to deal with what had become the stereotypical image of Liverpudlians. He and Dominic Behan had been billed to appear on the same TV programme. Dominic (1928–1989) was an Irish singer, professional Dubliner, songwriter, playwright and seasoned drinker, whose songs included the *Patriot Game*, telling of an incident in the IRA's uprising in the 1950s, and *Liverpool Lou*, a romantic ballad, which became a hit in 1974 for The Scaffold.

Dominic was the young brother of Brendan Behan (1923–1964). Brendan had been arrested in Liverpool in 1959 after police had been tipped off that he was carrying explosives with which he had intended blowing up the Cammell Laird shipyard in Birkenhead. This resulted in a three-year sentence, described in his autobiographical novel, *Borstal Boy*. Brendan eventually drank himself to death, but before that he had written the acclaimed plays, *The Hostage* and *The Quare Fellow*, on which his reputation now rest.

Anyway, Melly and Dominic Behan were in the same studio. This is how our man told me the story in a Liverpool pub: "It was a BBC programme called *Late Night Line-Up*, which was known among us as Late Night Booze-Up because its hospitality was always open. God, he (Behan) was drunk! He insisted on two things. The first one was that he thought some perfectly harmless lackey of the BBC was upper-class and he kept trying to kick him, missing each time. The other was that he was convinced that I, as a Liverpudlian, had been running about the city with my arse hanging out of my breeks. I couldn't persuade him that I had a middle-class upbringing and had my arse well within my breeks."

This, of course, was true, but George had been known to remove his clothing as a party performance, an example of his flamboyant behaviour, which was not appreciated by all. He was born and raised in a substantial Victorian house on the fringes of Sefton Park, Liverpool. Although his parents, Francis and Edith, were libertarians, family wealth in shipping and commerce kept them in style. George attended Stowe public school, before he served in the Merchant Navy as an able seaman between 1944 and 1947. Some of his experiences at sea are described in his early autobiography, *Rum, Bum and Concertina*.

Surrealistic art was his enduring passion, but he was perhaps better known as a jazz and blues singer with his magnificent, sherry trifle of a voice soaking and then rolling over the double-entendres. He first joined Mick Mulligan's Magnolia Jazz band during the New Orleans revival of the late 1940s and early 1950s. From the early 1970s until 2003, he was with John Clifton's Feetwarmers. Towards the end, he was singing with Digby Fairthweather's band. From 1956 until 1971, he wrote the captions for the *Daily Mail*'s Flook, a satirical cartoon strip drawn by Trog (Wally Fawkes). He also wrote on films, TV and pop music for *The Observer*. Melly was a showy dresser, favouring candy-striped suits and spats, but he had progressive political views and believed in the rights of man, while loathing those who would repress human desires.

When death was closing in, the conker-eyed Melly, grew a biblical beard, so that he would look like Christ returning to his father. By then he was suffering from cancer and dementia, which he mocked as a fitting disease for a surrealist. His going left a cavernous hole in British society. This great Liverpudlian, "Good Time" George, "Gorgeous" George, call him what you like, was a splendid eccentric – writer, wearer of hats, raconteur, singer, boozer, lover, gossip, outrager, smoker and the crusher of privet-hedge morality.

ELVIS PRESLEY (1935–1977) was the most popular entertainer in the world. He was born into poverty in Tupelo, Mississippi. His original recordings for the Sun label in Memphis, Tennessee, were very influential in spreading the popularity of rock and roll because, so it was said, he was a white man who sounded like a black man. His animated singing coupled with his good looks and his moody and sexy poses appealed greatly to The Beatles' generation, though many, including John Lennon, lamented the softer style that followed his two years in the US Army. The rebel had been tamed for mass consumption. Even so, like Lonnie Donegan and Buddy Holly, Elvis was a huge influence on Merseybeat. His surname is rarely used in conversation, making "Elvis" an international brand.

CILLA BLACK (1943–). In the early days of her fame, she was surprisingly gawky, the sort of girl that everyone liked, but she would not have been the obvious choice for a backstreet Romeo. People then thought of her as an updated version of Gracie Fields, the Lancashire lass with a comic bearing and a voice to tremble the chandeliers.

But to me Cilla seemed more like a working-class Joyce Grenfell. To those of you, unaccustomed to the English humour of the 1950s and '60s, Miss Grenfell was the perpetually engaged/never married policewoman from the St Trinian's films, possessed of kind eyes and egg-shelling teeth, whose Girl Guide walk swung from the hips in a love of jam and Jerusalem, as well as girls' boarding schools and morning mists and everything that was jolly decent.

But Priscilla Maria Veronica White was separated from the hockey fields by her upbringing next to a Chinese laundry on Scotland Road. Her father was a docker and her mother had a market-stall. But there was ambition in her parents, who appreciated the advantages of a good education and Cilla left St Anthony's School hoping for a steady, clerical job. Her chances of this happening were further enhanced by her time at Anfield Commercial College.

The young woman from the old Irish community of Liverpool, which had been settled by those fleeing the Potato Famine, became a typist like the thousands of other girls who perched on office stools. For most of them, the best hope of advancement in life lay in hooking Mr Right, but Cilla prayed for something more.

At night, she worked as the cloakroom girl in the Cavern Club on Mathew Street in the city centre. It was, of course, the jazz cellar that had become a home to an increasing number of skiffle and rock and roll groups, developing what would become the Mersey sound.

Cilla could sing, but apart from a few American girls, such as Brenda Lee and Carol King, men dominated the British charts. The exception was Helen Shapiro, whose ancestors were hard-working Russian Jews. Helen had been brought up in comparative poverty in Bethnal Green and then Hackney. So the two girls had in common a burning desire to improve their circumstances. In 1961, when she was only 14, Helen scored major hits with *You Don't Know* and *Walkin' Back to Happiness*. It could be done. A couple of years later the emerging Beatles supported her on a national tour, though by then they were an unstoppable force in pop music, while Helen had peaked.

Cilla, who knew The Beatles, began singing at the Iron Door Club on Temple Street, near the Cavern. She was exactly what Brian Epstein, new manager of The Beatles wanted – "the next Gracie Fields", a wholesome girl with a strong voice, who would appeal to all the family. Musical crazes come and go, but she had the qualities to last as an all-round entertainer and she certainly has lasted, still widely popular at a time when only local enthusiasts remember the names of many of her Merseybeat contemporaries.

But she does have a problem among some Liverpudlians. Late one night I was a guest on a Radio Merseyside chat show, hosted by Linda McDermott, who is one of the finest and most sympathetic broadcasters in local journalism, thanks to a prodigious knowledge of her native Liverpool and a truly sympathetic manner.

When we were off air, a fellow panellist said that she could never forgive Cilla for losing her Liverpool accent. This observation would come as a surprise to people outside the area, who would immediately associate Cilla with the Liverpool accent. It suggests that there is a celebrity or theatrical Liverpool accent, which is different to the real Scouse accent heard on the streets.

Indeed, the Liverpool accent has changed drastically in a comparatively short time. Listening to recordings of great Liverpool comedians from an earlier time, such as Arthur Askey, Ted Ray or Robb Wilton, or the comic actor Deryck Guyler, you are left with the impression of tones that are broadly northern rather than specifically Liverpudlian. To some extent, the same could be said of Ken Dodd.

The splendid Radio Merseyside presenter, Billy Butler, who was born in 1942 and, like Linda, has a voluminous knowledge of popular culture, is rightly proud of his Liverpool accent, but it is far less pronounced than those used by the present generation of Scouse celebrities.

In fact, it has become quite difficult to identify some Scouse accents. For example, there is a "posh" Liverpool voice, heard in such grand institutions as the city's revered Athenaeum, which has nothing in common with the street accent. My own theory is that during The Beatles' era the Liverpool accent became the most imitated in the country. As people were imitating stars, who were already exaggerating their accents to capitalize on the popularity of the city, a new Liverpool voice emerged.

Meanwhile, middle-class parents had sent their children to elocution lessons and private schools in the hope, often vain, that their children would not speak "like dat".

It seems to me that Cilla's speaking voice, with her catchphrase "lorra,

lorra", has been stretched this way and that, as she has adjusted her speech to suit particular audiences.

But there can be no doubt that she is a true Liverpool girl, who followed the common ambition of young women from her background, simply "to make good". After all, people from other occupations tune their voice slightly to accord with their company. This is a polite desire to fit in, rather than treachery.

In Liverpool, however, the decision to move away does cause resentment. Some see it as desertion. Cilla was also suspected of having Tory leanings, in common with many working-class people, who believed in prosperity from hard graft. But this was not popular during the late 1980s when Liverpool was suffering under the policies of Margaret Thatcher's Conservative government. Such antagonism softened in the twenty-first century, when Liverpool revived, leading to the 2008 European Capital of Culture year.

Despite that, however, there was still some carping when Cilla was cast as the Fairy Godmother in that year's panto at the Liverpool Empire. Inevitably, critics wanted to know how much she was being paid to return to her native city and there was speculation about her "prima donna" demands. In the end, though, it was her superb performance that won the day. Her singing voice, not always regarded as the finest instrument, won special praise for its new maturity.

One of Epstein's first managerial decisions with her had been a change of name from White to Black. It is difficult to know how much this helped, if at all. Anyway, her first record, *Love of the Loved*, scraped the charts in 1963, but she followed it with the Burt Bacharach/Hal David song, *Anyone Who Had a Heart*, which soared to number one. It's yearning for affection was perfect for a girl, who was not an out-and-out beauty, and she sang it with wonderful exuberance. With other big hits, including *You're My World* and *Alfie*, Cilla's singing career sustained remarkably well into the early 1970s and included a version of *You've Lost That Loving Feeling*. It reached number two before being eclipsed by the thunderous version from the Righteous Brothers, memorably arranged by Phil Spector and perhaps one of the finest rock/pop recordings ever made.

In 1969, Cilla had married talented local boy Bobby Willis, who had himself been a singer and a budding songwriter, but he devoted the rest of his life to guiding her career. He died from cancer in 1999, leaving Cilla devastated. By then she was one of the most popular entertainers on TV.

In 1968, a year after Epstein's death, his long-term hopes for her had begun to be realised when she was given her own show, *Cilla*, which opened with the song, *Step Inside Love*, written for her by Paul McCartney. A strong line-up of guests helped to make it a big success and it opened the way to her mainstream TV family shows *Surprise, Surprise* (1984–2001) and *Blind Date* (1985–2003).

Unlike some Merseybeat stars, Cilla never rested on past achievements. When times were tough, she worked in the cabaret clubs. In 1994, students protested against her being awarded an honorary degree by the Liverpool John Moores University, but they didn't understand how much courage it takes to walk on a stage. Behind the scenes, there were tragedies in Cilla's life, but, with rare resolution, she had risen from Scotland Road to the heights of showbiz. In truth, she is not to everyone's taste, but she is a Great Liverpudlian.

GERRY MARSDEN (1942–). There is a throaty and soulful quality in his voice, the suggestion of phlegm not quite cleared, which gives it an instant identity with fans on the football terraces.

The song, *You'll Never Walk Alone*, is a tear-squeezer from the 1945 Rodgers and Hammerstein musical, *Carousel*. In the second act, Nettie Fowler, the cousin of the female protagonist Julie Jordan, sings the song to comfort Julie, whose husband, Billy Bigelow, the male lead, has killed himself after a failed robbery. It is sung again in the final scene to encourage a graduation class of which Louise (their daughter) is a member. Billy attends this ceremony during his ghostly return to Earth, inspiring them with words of encouragement and assuring them of his love. As a result of this, *You'll Never Walk Alone*, became a favourite at American graduation ceremonies. There is a strength in the song's message that rises above slushy sentimentality, giving it a quality similar to a revivalist hymn. Many famous people, including Elvis Presley and Frank Sinatra, have sung it, often in an operatic style, but Gerry seemed instinctively to appreciate its keener quality. Almost invariably on hearing someone else's version, people say, "Yes, but I still prefer Gerry singing it".

Gerry and his brother Freddie (1940–2006) were born into a devoted working-class family in Liverpool's Dingle district. Their father, Fred, worked on the railways and their mother, Mary, was a school cleaner and an assistant in a fish and chip shop. From an early age, Gerry seemed a likely lad, bright, witty enough to survive the hurly-burly on the playground at Mount Carmel school, a promising footballer and boxer with the looks that would have made him an instant "cheeky chappy" at any casting agency. In common with thousands of other boys from his generation, he was caught up in Lonnie Donegan's skiffle craze. Its appeal soon eclipsed that of the 7th Toxteth Scouts and, with a guitar bought by his dad, Gerry formed a skiffle group, which played at all the usual local venues. Nonetheless, there wasn't sufficient money for him to give up his day jobs, which included spells on coal delivery, making tea chests and van deliveries. But his talent was obvious. After a while, he called his group Gerry and the Mars Bars, but objections from the manufacturers of the famous chocolate confection led to the formation of Gerry and the Pacemakers.

Students of pop music's sociology might note that most of the great British groups did not highlight one member – The Beatles, Kinks, Rolling Stones, Searchers, Hollies, Animals and so on. Of course, there are some exceptions, but this does suggest that, from an early age, Gerry accepted that he was the star. The group secured bookings at Liverpool's Cavern Club and before long, like The Beatles and others, they were performing in Hamburg. This apprenticeship stood them in good stead. Brian Epstein, manager of The Beatles, signed the Pacemakers in 1962, six months after he had acquired The Beatles. Epstein knew that The Beatles were his prize asset, but Gerry's serious recording career began with three straight number ones – *How Do You Do It? I Like It* and *You'll Never Walk Alone*, all in 1963.

If Epstein had been an old-fashioned pop manager, he would probably have judged The Beatles and Pacemakers to be equals from whom he would have to wring the maximum money before the public lost interest. He understood, however, that The Beatles were special and that Gerry and the Pacemakers, though splendid entertainers, would not be at the forefront of the social changes and liberal attitudes that marked the 1960s as the most significant post-war decade. Even so, they continued to be a major chart act with songs such as *I'm the One* and the wonderful *Don't Let the Sun Catch Your Crying*, both penned by Gerry with help from other members of the group.

Despite their Liverpool accents, which could be exaggerated or diminished to suit the occasion, The Beatles were quickly a national and then an international phenomenon. This distanced them from their Merseybeat origins. By contrast, Gerry and his Pacemakers (brother Freddie on the drums, Les Maguire, piano, and Les Chadwick, guitar) clung on to their Liverpool roots, as London gradually regained its position as Britain's pop music capital. The 1965 film, *Ferry 'Cross the Mersey*, starring Gerry and the Pacemakers, Cilla Black, the Fourmost, the Black Knights, Earl Royce and the Olympics and the Blackwells, was released just in time, though it is now a largely forgotten period piece.

The title song, written by Gerry and a hit on both sides of the Atlantic, was to prove more important. With this song, Gerry, who settled in Wirral, expressed his enduring devotion to Merseyside. This was officially recognised by his being granted the freedom of Liverpool in 2009.

Gerry and the Pacemakers broke up in 1967, as the decade was about to turn psychedelic. He began a solo career and the following year starred in the musical *Charley Girl*.

Yet people would never forget the haunting way he had sung *You'll Never Walk Alone*, his voice adding a rare passion to the lush playing of the orchestra. The song became a favourite on the Kop and was adopted by Liverpool Football Club as its official anthem. The supporters of other football clubs clubs also sang it, but without that special fervour. Everton's Goodison Park was about the only ground, where it wasn't heard – until the Gwladys Street enders came up with their own mocking version, which swapped "walk on, walk on" for the rudest two-word dismissal in the English language, and then made a brief reference to soap and bottoms, before ending "you'll never walk again".

However, the true song has been sung by Gerry in times of high emotion. In 1974, he performed it in Liverpool Cathedral at the memorial service for Bill Shankly. The song's anthemic quality would be heard again in 1989. On April 15, an event had shaken the whole nation. It is recorded in history with two words, the Hillsborough Disaster. Ninety-six Liverpool fans died as the result of a crush at the Leppings Road end of Sheffield Wednesday's ground, Hillsborough, where Liverpool had begun playing Nottingham Forest in a semi-final of the FA Cup. Such profound mourning had never before been experienced in peace-time Britain. On the same day, Everton had beaten Norwich City in the other semi-final. So the final at Wembley was a derby match, totally overwhelmed by the feelings of a grieving city.

Gerry sang *Ferry 'Cross the Mersey* and *You'll Never Walk Alone* to the huge crowd. His devotion to his native city in times of trouble will always be remembered. Maybe without *You'll Never Walk Alone*, he would have been simply a very fine summer show and panto star, like so many of his contemporaries. But that song made Gerry Marsden a very Great Liverpudlian.

GRACIE FIELDS (1898–1979). "Our Gracie" was a popular singer, actress and comedienne. Some said that Brian Epstein had her in mind when he groomed Cilla Black for stardom. Gracie was born above a fish and chip shop in Rochdale. Her big hits, sung at a piercing pitch, include *Sally, Sing as We Go, Now is the Hour* and *The Biggest Aspidistra in the World*. A huge crowd watched her open the magnificent 2,500-seat Ritz Cinema (later the Essoldo Ritz) in Birkenhead in 1937. Twenty-one years later, Billy Fury was discovered at a rock and roll show in the cinema, which was demolished in 2000.

GENE VINCENT (1935–1971) was an early rock and roller, who scored a big hit with the self-penned *Be-Bop-A-Lula*. He had served with the US Navy in Korea. A motorbike accident seriously injured his left leg, but added to his sullen stance and prowling limp on stage, wearing black leathers. As a rock rebel, he had some influence on Merseybeat groups.

EDDIE COCHRAN (1938–1960) was a fine American guitarist and rock and roller, much admired by the emerging Merseybeat groups. His big hits include the self-composed *Summertime Blues, C'mon Everybody, Something Else* and *Three Steps to Heaven*. On April 16, 1960, he was travelling in a Ford Consul taxi in Chippenham, Wiltshire. It hit a lamp-post. Eddie died from his injuries. Early death added to his mystique. His friend Gene Vincent and the songwriter Sharon Sheeley were also injured in the crash, but survived.

BUDDY HOLLY (1936–1959, born in Lubbock, Texas) was rock and roll's first genius and, after Lonnie Donegan and Elvis Presley, the greatest influence on Merseybeat groups, including The Beatles and The Searchers.

With his group, the Crickets, Holly played in what became the standard rock and roll line-up of two guitars, a bass and drums. On March 20, 1958, he performed in the wonderful acoustics and art deco surrounds of the Liverpool Philharmonic Hall. Although The Beatles Lennon, McCartney and Harrison were not there, some of their friends were at the concert. Seeing Holly that night persuaded dozens of Mersey groups that skiffle was finished. The future was rock and roll. To celebrate the importance of the occasion, a 50th memorial concert at the Phil featured interpretations of Holly songs by many local stars.

On February 2, 1959, Holly and his fellow performers, Richie Valens and JP "the Big Bopper" Richardson had chartered a Beechcraft Bonanza aeroplane. Shortly after take-off it crashed killing them all and the 21-year-old pilot, Roger Peterson. It was the saddest moment in the young history of rock and roll. From that point on, people understood more clearly the dangers of what became known as the music's lifestyle. The news was greeted with great sorrow in Liverpool. But the mood of that time was not fully expressed until 1971 when *American Pie (the Day the Music Died)* became a hit for the American singer/songwriter, Don McLean.

Holly's great songs include *That'll be the Day*, *Peggy Sue*, *Peggy Sue Got Married*, *Rave On*, *Maybe Baby*, *Not Fade Away*, *Oh Boy* and *True Love Ways*.

LONNIE DONEGAN (1931–2002). It would have been impossible for him to count all his children, but Lonnie was the "father" of the skiffle craze, which swept Britain in the late mid and late 1950s. Thousands of teenagers followed his example and started playing "skiffle" music, which in England meant singing American folk songs very fast to the accompaniment of guitars, drums and mouth-organs. Some of the earlier groups used homemade double basses. At their most primitive, a broom handle would be secured in a large tea chest with a string attached to it. This would be slapped and plucked by its enthusiastic owner. Thimbled and often skilled fingers ran up and down washboards to build-up the frenzied rhythm. In fact, most of the more advanced groups quickly swapped their washboards for drums, but, in the folk memory of those days, the washboard became an essential instrument.

Ironically, their popularity coincided with the arrival of the first washing machines in many British homes. All the famous British groups of the

1960s – The Beatles, Rolling Stones, Kinks, the Animals and so on – freely acknowledged their debt to Donegan and his fellow skifflers. Young curates, who had until then expressed their devotion to God by playing ping-pong with juvenile delinquents, began growing beards over their pimples. Before long skiffle groups were crunching down the gravel paths, by the latticed windows of suburbia's sandstone churches, where they were to play their songs to bemused members of the congregation, who squirmed on the pews and wished that the organist would press out the familiar strains of *O Happy Band of Pilgrims* or *Immortal, Invisible, God only Wise*.

Although it was perhaps not evident to everyone, Donegan's songs were drawn from the labour camps and plantations of America. Most had been written by Huddie Ledbetter (Leadbelly) or Woody Guthrie. To that extent the curates were right to invite the skiffle groups into the churches and youth clubs in the hope of making religion "relevant" to young people. Sentiments in the songs could be lost in the frantic delivery, but *Pick a Bale of Cotton* and *Bring A Little Water Sylvie* were about the plight of black slaves in the Deep South while *John Henry*, *Ramblin' Round*, *The Grand Coulee Dam* and *The Rock Island Line* were also work songs. They provided a generation of teenagers with an alternative history of America.

All these songs were familiar to the boys in Liverpool's emerging music scene, including, of course, Paul McCartney, John Lennon, George Harrison and Ringo Starr. For a while Donegan was their hero and mentor.

He had been born in Glasgow, the son of an impecunious violinist, who had played in the Scottish National Orchestra. In the Hungry Thirties, not long after the birth of Anthony James Donegan, the family moved to East Ham in London. "Tony", as his family and friends called him, loved music from his boyhood, particularly jazz, country and western and the music hall songs of the day. By the late 1940s, he had a decent reputation as a guitarist, though it was as a banjo player that he joined Chris Barber's Jazz band. Donegan's career was interrupted by National Service with the Army, which in 1949 took him to Vienna, then emerging like a ghost from the ruins of war. There he met American servicemen, who widened his taste in music. On his returns home, Donegan introduced these songs and some were included in the Barber repertoire.

Much later, Donegan described the atmosphere of those times.

"In England, we were separated from our folk music tradition centuries ago and were imbued with the idea that music was for the upper classes. You had to be very clever to play music. When I came along with the old three chords, people began to think that if I could do it, so could they. It was the reintroduction of the folk music bridge which did that."

At a concert at the Royal Festival Hall in London, the compere introduced his as Lonnie Donegan, confusing his name with the fine bluesman Lonnie Johnson, who was on the same bill. The name stuck.

The benefit of Donegan's devotion to America folk/skiffle songs came to fruition at a recording session for Chris Barber's 1954 LP *New Orleans Joy*, which included Lonnie Donegan performing the Rock Island line. In 1956, it was released as a single and became a major hit on both sides of the Atlantic.

In 1958, Paul McCartney saw Donegan, then at the height of his popularity perform at the Liverpool Empire.

A year earlier the Cavern Club had opened in Mathew Street Liverpool. Originally a jazz club, it would also feature skiffle and then beat groups, despite the raised brows and sulks of the musical purists. But Donegan was too big a star to appear in concert at such a small venue with its sweating brick walls, evil-smelling lavatories and rude youths. However, he did go there to sing a few songs and meet members of the local branch of his fan club, including its secretary Tony Davis, who would later be a star in his own right as the "tall one" in the Spinners (Davis, Mick Groves, Hughie Jones and Cliff Hall), a Liverpool folk group that specialised in shanties and songs promoting racial harmony. The session was apparently interrupted by a group of young men in leather jackets, who were practising their own songs. Donegan had to ask them to "keep it down". It has since been suggested, perhaps a little fancifully, that they were the Quarrymen, who would later become The Beatles. Who knows?

In 1962, Donegan had his last hit with *Pick a Bale of Cotton* and The Beatles had their first with *Love Me Do*.

Despite the immense energy of Lonnie, who also had the strut and the guitar-pose of a cool dude, skiffle burned out. Its wide acceptance by middle-class students protesting against the bomb, as well as the ginger-bearded folkies, distanced it from the city boys and girls, who would take up rock and roll, adapting it into beat and the rhythm and blues, which made the British groups of the 1960s the most popular in the world.

Donegan's credibility had been further damaged by his recording of the massively successful novelty numbers, *Does Your Chewing Gum Lose its Flavour?* and *My Old Man's a Dustman*.

But The Beatles never forgot the influence he had on their careers. "He was the first person we had heard of from Britain to get to the coveted number one in the charts, and we studied his records avidly. We all bought guitars to be in a skiffle group. He was the man," said McCartney.

And Lonnie wasn't finished with Liverpool. Two years before his death he was invited to make his proper debut at the Cavern. More than 400 people packed the cellar to see him give a magnificent performance. He was 70 and deserved his reputation as the Grand Old Man of British Rock. He had been awarded the MBE that year.

"Not before time," said Prince Charles at the ceremony. "You're damn right, sir," replied Lonnie.

With the bravery of the true and incorrigible showman, he had ignored medical advice to take it easy and protect his over-strained heart. Before that performance, we had a long chat in a local café. Lonnie was not a modest man, though I liked him very much. "All roads lead to Lonnie," he said. He was right.

This man, whose contribution to popular culture surely makes him an honorary Liverpudlian, died in the midst of a national tour, prophetically called This Could Be The Last Time.

RON FORMBY (1946–) has dedicated much of his adult career to ensuring that the part played by the old communities is never forgotten in the history of Liverpool. He must also be praised for giving us the word "quangoesque" to describe the bumptious and often useless individuals, who attach themselves to publicly-funded or sponsored organisations dedicated to the notion that every problem can be solved by a meeting or a conference or a seminar or an away day.

"You're not from round here, are you?" is the question from Ron that they dread, but if he does detect a genuine desire to learn, he will go to immense lenths to help them.

In 1989, after working in shipping offices and shops, Ron arrived at the Vauxhall Neighbourhood Council, which served the old Scotland Road area, from a building in Silvester Street. His intention was to study for an English O level. Before long, however, he was working for the monthly Scottie Press community newspaper, which is read by most families in the area, as well as by those who have settled in Canada, the USA, Australia, New Zealand and various parts of Britain. What good is a qualification in English, if you don't use it?

Ron's father Bill was a telephonist and his mother Pat was a factory worker. He was brought up in Pansy Street, Kirkdale.

In common with many Great Liverpudlians, young Ron was a fine guitarist and the singer of songs, but his abiding sorrow was the destruction of the old Liverpool communities and their replacement with soulless high-rise flats and out-of-town estates.

There was nothing he liked better than to see men and women gathered in a pub or bingo hall discussing the ways of the world. Everybody knew eveybody and when that happened people didn't go astray. Of course, some did but the sense of decency in the community prevented that happening as often as it does now. If you have run out of sugar, why shouldn't you pop next door to borrow some? And while you are there, why not have a chat about young Tony, who is turning into a bit of a tearaway, or Veronica, whose skirts are very short. To Ron, this was civilization at its highest – people looking after each other. To this end, he had devoted himself tirelessly to the promotion of community activities such as reunions, photographic exhibitions, down Memory Lane talks and so on.

He remembers with yearning the times when you could walk into a pub within minutes be engaged in a conversation about space travel or the advantages of a tricycle over a bicycle.

Although he has suffered from ill-health of late, Ron is a guitarist, an superb photographer and a magnificent conversationalist, whose contribution to Liverpool has been immeasurable.

GODFREY CARNEY (1909–2008) possessed the finest qualities of the hundreds of the Irish-born priests, who have served communities in Liverpool since the Irish Potato Famine.

In addition to his unwavering devotion to the traditional teachings of the church, Father Carney was a towering intellect and a lyrical speaker, who could hold congregations spellbound. He wrote poems and short stories of wit and understanding, suggesting that he could he could have trod the literary trails of Sean O'Casey, James Joyce, Brendan Behan and many of his fellow countrymen blessed with a gift for words. Instead, he devoted himself to the Roman Catholic faith.

Some years before he died, he recalled his first impressions of Liverpool. "It was a very crowded place, very tightly packed. There were a lot of factories and smoke and grime. On a hot day the tanneries would smell like fury and there was a sugar house, a feather-bed factory, all sorts of things."

He was sorry that the faith had weakened in Liverpool and his native Ireland, but he remembered when, "the faith was deep and the sacraments came to us like drawing breath, like sleeping".

THOMAS STEERS (1672–1750) was a Kent-born civil engineer, who served with William of Orange (1650–1702) at the Battle of the Boyne. In 1710, he began building an embankment across the south side of the tidal inlet known in Liverpool as the Pool. It was opened in 1715 in a site near the present Canning Place, starting the great network of docks in the Port of Liverpool. The Pool was eventually completely filled in by docks and other developments.

QUEEN VICTORIA (1819–1901). Liverpool grew into the second port of the British Empire during her reign. But it was not until 1880 that Liverpool became a city. Much of the city's grandest architecture carried the confidence of the Victorian age.

PERCY FRENCH (1854–1920) was a brilliant Irish songwriter, entertainer and painter. He was born in Clooniquin, County Roscommon.

After a prolonged and jolly period studying civil engineering at Trinity College, Dublin, he became an inspector of drains, seeing in this activity the potential for much comic writing and storytelling. It was as the writer and performer of funny songs, a gentle mockery of Irish life, that he established his reputation. But he is most fondly remembered for *The Mountains of Mourne*, which became the hymn for Irish people making their livings in England, but yearning for home and those mountains that sweep down to the sea. It is written to Mary by her sweetheart, who finds London a wonderful sight with everyone digging for gold in the street, but it could never be home. The same sentiment would have applied to Liverpool.

French's comic songs include *Phil the Fluther's Ball*, *Slattery's Mounted Foot* and *Are Ye Right There Michael?* (about the railways in County Clare). Indignant rail officials took French to court, feeling that he had defamed their reputation, but the man himself was late for the hearing because, it is said, he travelled by train.

French was taken ill in Glasgow and then stayed with his cousin Canon John Brooke Richardson in Formby, where he died several days later. He is buried there in St Luke's churchyard, Formby, which has become a place of pilgrimage.

SIR HENRY TATE (1819–1899) was a Chorley-born sugar refiner and patron of the arts. He gave Britain the Tate Gallery (the Tate Liverpool, which specialises in modern art opened on the Albert Dock in 1988). He bought the patent on a method of cutting sugar into cubes in 1872 and opened his great Liverpool refinery on Love Lane in the same year. In 1898, he was made a baronet.

ABRAM LYLE (1820–1891) was a Scottish businessman and sugar refiner, particularly famed for Golden Syrup. In 1921, the company he had begun merged with that of Henry Tate to form Tate & Lyle. Tate had established a refinery in Love Lane, Liverpool in 1872. Its closure in 1981 excited much sorrow and anger in Liverpool.

ALAN BLEASDALE (1946–) is a writer of passion, wit and sincerity, who crafted one of the finest jokes in British drama for his TV series, *Boys from the Black Stuff*, which charts the miseries suffered by Yosser Hughes (Bernard Hill) during the recession of the 1980s. In a state of total despair, Yosser enters the confession box at a church. On the other side is the priest, Father Daniel Thomas (Struan Rodger).

"I'm desperate, father," says Yosser.
"It can be a desperate world at times," Mr Hughes.

Yosser asks the priest to call him Yosser.

"It can be a desperate world at times, Yosser Hughes" says the priest, who can hear sobbing on the other side.

"Tell me, would it make any difference if ... a trouble shared in a place of peace, my son ... a haven. I am Father Thomas. Doubting Thomas for short."

There is no response to this joke, so the priest repeats it. "Doubting Thomas", but then adds "Daniel Thomas. Daniel. Don't worry about the father. Call me Dan."

Yosser: "I'm desperate, Dan,"

Then realising what he has just said, Yosser head-butts the Cross on the wall, knocking it off its nail.

Everything was timed to perfection in that scene. But the five episodes of the series were a triumph of dark humour, sentiment and anger, telling of the effect of unemployment on a group of tar-layers (hence the title) and their families and friends.

Bleasdale was brought up in Huyton and Widnes and qualified as a teacher. His first literary success came in the early 1970s with a scally schoolboy called Scully, whose adventures he read on local radio. The character would later be developed for a play, two novels and a TV series.

When Liverpool was designated as the 2008 European Capital of Culture, I asked Alan if it would be good for the city. "Ask me again in 2009," he said, suggesting that the benefits might not filter down to the ordinary people. At the time such an opinion was almost heresy, though many might now think of it as prophetic.

With his thick black eyebrows meeting in the middle and his formidable, if slightly grizzled beard, Bleasdale has the bearing of a Russian writer of the joke-free school, but he really loves humorous discourses, which often involve the supposed failings of his own health.

Football was his greatest love as a young man and he had dreamed of playing for Liverpool. Instead he has had to make do with writing about the city.

His other plays include *Down the Dock Road*, *Fat Harold and the Last 26*, *Having a Ball*, *No Surrender* and *The Party's Over*. Most of his plays mix bleak humour with dramatic moments, underpinned by human anxiety.

A slight departure was *Are You Lonesome Tonight?* (1985), an examination of the last days of his hero, Elvis Presley.

DAVID SHEPPARD (1929–2005) was first seen as a handsome and dashing figure of immense charm, who enjoyed an education at Sherborne public school and then Cambridge, where he was a cricketing blue, on his way to stardom as a batsman with Sussex and England.

In later life, though, he was admired as a clergyman deeply committed to the easing of poverty, particularly in urban communities. It is certainly true that his sporting prowess and good looks made some doubt his true devotion to the causes that he espoused, but Sheppard overcame these doubts by sheer hard work and force of personality.

However, it should also be said that he was a very fine cricketer in the 1950s and 1960s. He played in 230 first class matches scoring 15,838 runs at an average of 43.51. He played in 22 test matches, scoring 1,172 runs at an average of 37.80.

Cricket fans knew that he had been ordained into the Church of England in 1955, but most then were more interested in his form at the crease, rather than the Cross.

He retired from test cricket in 1963 and six years later was appointed Bishop of Woolwich. By the time he was appointed Bishop of Liverpool in 1975, he was an experienced broadcaster and writer in the popular *Press*, as well as more lofty journals.

Much of his time in the city was dedicated to the poor of the city, whose circumstances greatly worsened during the recession of the 1970s and 1980s. He felt that Margaret Thatcher's Conservative government was totally out of touch with feelings in a city, where thousands had lost their jobs on the docks and in the factories.

Tensions between the Roman Catholic and Protestant communities, which once led to riots and bitter fighting on Orange marches, had been lessening for years – through lethargy as much as good faith. But Sheppard's friendship with the Catholic Archbishop of Liverpool, Derek Worlock, led to the Anglican and Catholic communities uniting in their passion to help Liverpool.

But three major events further damaged the reputation of the city in Britain. The first happened at the Heysel Stadium, near Brussels, where Liverpool were playing Juventus in the European Cup Final in May 1985. Ill-feeling between the fans boiled over before the kick-off when a charge by Liverpool supporters resulted in a dividing wall collapsing. Thirty nine Italians were killed and hundreds more injured, as they retreated. Subsequent entreaties by the Liverpools fans that the Italians had not been entirely blameless for the carnage were largely ignored.

Then in 1989 came the Hillsborough Disaster, which resulted in 96 deaths. While the city mourned, newspapers, particularly *The Sun*, were wrongly blaming the Liverpool supporters for their own tragedy.

In February 1993, James Bulger was led from the New Strand Shopping Centre, Bootle, by two 10-year-old boys. They took him to the side of a rail track about two miles away in Walton. There James, who was not quite three, was tortured and murdered. Grief and anger spread across the country. Middle-class journalists were shocked by what they found in Liverpool. They couldn't, of course, blame the city for the murder, but it had happened here. Soon the innocent face of James and pictures of the miseries and dereliction of Liverpool merged into a continuous nightmare, which reached into the soul.

In this adversity the city united and closed in on itself. Liverpudlians raised a collective shield. Enough was enough. What about all the good things the city had given Britain? Did they count for nothing now?

It was in this new mood of defiance that Liverpool's recovery began. As a man of compassion and sympathy, Bishop Sheppard played a huge part in that.

DEREK WORLOCK (1920–1996). When he was Archbishop of Liverpool, Derek Worlock formed such a close association with the Anglican Bishop David Sheppard that people likened them to Tweedledum and Tweedledee, though some preferred Fish and Chips, without specifying who was what.

Despite his gentle eyes and apparently diffident manner, Worlock could be an unyielding and authorative figure, well practised in the strangely ruthless world of church politics. He was born in London and educated at St Edmund's College from 1934 until 1944 when he was ordained.

For 19 years, Worlock was secretary to three successive Archbishops of Westminster – Bernard Griffin, Thomas Godfrey and John Heenan. He was appointed Bishop of Portsmouth in 1965 and served as Archbishop of Liverpool from 1976 until his death.

From the start, he was enthusiastic about closer ties with the other Christian denominations in Liverpool and to this end worked closely with Sheppard. Both men were convinced that Margaret Thatcher's government should have done more to help Liverpool during the recession of the 1980s, which was in part reposnisble for the rioting that broke out in the Toxteth area in the summer of 1981.

Worlock's triumph of that period was the part he played in the shadows to ensure that the proposed visit of Pope John Paul II would go ahead in 1982. Influential voices in the Vatican felt it should be called off as a protest against the war being waged by the United Kingdom and Argentina over the sovereignty of the Falkland Islands. Worlock helped broker the compromise, which meant the Pope visited Argentina later in the year.

During his visit to Liverpool, the Pope made history by stepping into the Anglican Cathedral, where he said the Lord's Prayer, before he travelled down Hope Street to says Mass in the Metropolitan Cathedral of Christ the King. Hundreds of thousands of Christians of all denominations had lined the Pope's seven-mile route from Liverpool Airport to the cathedrals. The visit was a triumph. For a few hours Liverpool was the heart of Christendom.

Quiet, scholarly and unwavering, Worlock formed a strong partnership with the better-known Sheppard. In 2007, Stephen Broadbent's statue of the two men, paid for by the public and organised by the *Liverpool Echo* newspaper, was unveiled on Hope Street.

KING JOHN (1167–1216) was often cruel, brutal, incompetent and given to rages of a Hitlerian magnitude. You might, therefore, have expected to find him listed in a book called Great Mancunians.

Well, yes – but the chap, though never a fully-fledged Scouser, had a crucial part to play in the development of Liverpool. He was also surnamed Lackland, which was appropriate enough for a man who succeeded in losing nearly all his French possessions – a remarkable feat given the quality of the opposition.

But here he is remembered for the Royal Charter of 1207 (known to local historians by its correct name of the Letters Patent), which established Liverpool as a port. It meant that people were induced to settle and develop businesses in Liverpool. His agents also laid out the original seven streets of Liverpool. These are Castle Street, Dale Street, Bank (now Water) Street, Juggler (High) Street, Chapel Street, Moor Street and Whiteacre (Old Hall) Street. He was also responsible for the development of the Royal Hunting Park, which extended over a vast area of Toxteth and Dingle now bordered by Upper Parliament Street, Smithdown Road and a stretch of the waterfront. Away from Liverpool, John's dealings were less happy. He became king in 1199 and four years later had his nephew Arthur murdered, lest he should have made a move for the throne. Despite his reputation as a "bad king", John was on occasions capable of bravery and decisive action. His problem was that he was very quarrelsome and his wars with Scotland and France drained the country's resources. When he was at a low ebb, the barons forced his to sign the Magna Carta (the Great Charter) in 1215 at Runnymede. It established legal rights for ordinary men and the liberty of the church among its many reforms. He died the following year.

© LIVERPOOL RECORD OFFICE, LIVERPOOL LIBRARIES AND INFORMATION SERVICES

HENRY FITZWARIN was a Norman landowner. In 1207, King John acquired some of his land in Liverpool, inviting people to settle on it and thus extend the small fishing port as an embarkation point for Ireland.

WALTER CARRUTHERS SELLAR (1898–1951) was a Scottish humourist and co-author with Robert Julian Yeatman of *1066 and All That*, an hilarious history of England, which lampooned our monarchs and leaders, including King John, though not for his part in founding Liverpool. However, their unflattering picture of John has endured rather better than any formal depiction of his character.

ROBERT JULIAN YEATMAN (1897–1968) was a British humourist awarded the MC for gallantry in the Great War. He was co-author with Walter Carruthers Sellar of *1066 and All That*, which poked fun at King John and many others. Although not Liverpudlians themselves Sellar and Yeatman gave us an unforgettable image of King John, foaming at the mouth and biting rushes, this man who granted us his Royal Charter.

PRINCE RUPERT (1619–1682) was appointed Commander of Horse by Charles I during the English Civil War. He epitomised the supposed romance of the Royalist cause, his bold escapades winning him the sobriquet of the Mad Cavalier. He successfully stormed Liverpool Castle in 1644, prising the small port from Parliamentary control. However, it was regained by John Moore's Roundheads. After the defeat of the Royalists, Rupert continued fighting dubious causes, often with the French against the English. However, he returned to England after the Restoration and helped develop an improved type of gunpowder called "Prince's Metal".

CHARLES I (1600–1649) was King of England and Ireland, but lost his throne and his head after the English Civil War. Liverpool was the centre of intense fighting. With control of the castle and port switching between the Royalists and the Parliamentarians. The castle was badly damaged, which contributed to its eventual demolition.

CHARLES II (1630–1685) was the son of Charles I. When the tide turn against the Royalists in the English Civil War, he was exiled and spent much of his time in France. He assumed the title of King on his father's execution, but did not become the monarch in fact until the Restoration 11 years later. He then had the troops removed from Liverpool Castle and ordered its partial demolition.

OLIVER CROMWELL (1599–1658), Lord Protector of the Commonwealth and leader of the Parliamentarians in the English Civil War, during which Liverpool Castle was captured by Prince Rupert and his Cavaliers in 1644. It was regained for Cromwell's cause by Sir John Moore.

JOHN MOORE (1599–1650) was a Member of Parliament for Liverpool in the early 1640s and had established shipping links in the port.

On the outbreak of the English Civil War in 1642, he sided with the Parliamentarians, in common with many Liverpool landowners, many of whom were from Puritan families. But the Royalists, including Liverpool's Mayor, John Walker, controlled the castle and its tower. The town was handed over to Lord Derby for the King. But in May 1643 Colonel John Moore and the Parliamentarians seized it for the loss of only seven men while killing 80 Royalists and capturing 300.

In gratitude, Cromwell made Moore a colonel and governor of Liverpool. Interestingly, though, Liverpool was not solid in its support of Parliament. Perhaps we can see shades here of the divisions still found in a city, which has always been drawn to the romance of money and glamour.

Wherever you look in Liverpool, particularly among the monuments, plaques and statues, you will see celebrations of the rich and famous, as well as the stones, poems, books and songs, which commemorate the struggles of the poor and oppressed. It is a strange mix.

As Moore was settling into his new role, Prince Rupert with 10,000 men was preparing to retake the city for the King, which he did in June 1664, killing some 1,500 Cromwellians. But Moore and some of his troops escaped across the Pool. When Sir John Meldrum's Parliamentary forces recaptured the city six months later, Moore was reappointed governor. Moore helped arrange the security for the King's trial. He was also a signatory on his death warrant in 1649. Moore later fought in Ireland, where he died of fever. Sometimes now I look into the faces of Liverpudlians, wondering if they would have been Roundheads or Cavaliers.

WILLIAM III (1650–1702) was King of Great Britain and Ireland. His soldiers used Liverpool Castle as an embarkation point for a campaign in Ireland in 1688.

GEORGE I (1660–1772) was King of Great Britain and Ireland. Liverpool Castle had fallen into a hopeless state of repair and in 1784, he gave the site to the Mayor and Corporation of Liverpool at an annual rent of £6 13s and 4d (£6.67). St George's Church was built there and then rebuilt before work began on the Victoria monument in 1902.

WILLIAM HESKETH LEVER (1851–1925), the first Viscount Leverhulme. Soap made the man and the man made soap.

Every time you pick up a cake of scented soap in your bathroom think of this man. Small in stature but big in ambition, he became the world's most successful soap manufacturer, whose workers lived in the mock Tudor splendour of Port Sunlight village. Lever was born in Bolton. He left school at 15 to join his fathers's grocery business, which he helped expand. In 1854, he married local girl and his long-time sweetheart, Elizabeth Ellen Hulme, at St George's Congregational Church, Bolton, the denomination that he supported all his life.

An early brainwave of his was pre-cutting and packaging soap, which had until then been cut from slabs on the grocer's counter. He registered one of his products as Sunlight. With his brother, James, who would play a much smaller part in the story, Lever leased a factory in Warrington to make soap that would appeal to housewives. In 1888, William, Ellen and their son, William Hulme Lever, moved to Thornton Manor, Wirral. By then he was a prosperous man, but, in common with so many Victorians, he had a grander vision, which he would express in 1906.

"A child, who knows nothing about God's earth, of green fields, of sparkling brooks, of breezy hill and springy heather, and whose mind is stored with none of the beauties of nature, but knows only the drunkenness prevalent in the hideous slums it is forced to live in, and whose walks abroad have never extended beyond the corner public house and the pawnship cannot be benefited by education. Such children grow up depraved and become a danger to the state; wealth-destroyers instead of wealth-producers."

This sentiment tell us much about Lever. He was the true paternalist, who believed that his good works would yield their own reward. His grandest vision was Port Sunlight village, built around his factory. In 1857, he had bought a 56-acre stretch of land at £200 an acre, much of it was marsh cut by ravines. Despite this, he continued buying and soon had 221 acres, 130 of which became the village. In 1889, 28 houses were ready for occupancy at rents of five shillings (25p) and eight shillings and ninepence (43p), depending on whether they had three or four bedrooms. The condition was that you had to be an employee of Lever Brothers to have one. In 1894, Lever Brothers became a public company. Two years earlier, Lever had stood as a Liberal MP for Birkenhead. He lost, but he was elected as the party's MP for Wirral in 1906. His wife, a tiny and tolerant woman, died in 1913. "I am convinced that without her great influence there would have been neither a Port Sunlight or a Lever Brothers," he said.

It was to her memory that he dedicated the "Taj Mahal" of Port Sulight, the Lady Lever Gallery, which was opened by George V in 1922, the year that he was raised to the peerage, combining their names to Leverhulme.

"What I want this and the succeeding generations to know as they contemplate this building and its treasures, is that they are the creation not of genius, but of hard-plodding work within the reach of all those who want to make the necessary sacrifice. And the inspiration to me has been the wife, I was fortunate enough to win. It has been truly said that a man, who has the good luck to win the hand of a good woman, has won everything life can give," he said.

Some may sense in all this gushing praise that the little girlfriend of his youth had become a symbol of womanhood, rather than his wife. Did he feel that he had dedicated more time to his business than to her? If so, did her view the beautiful gallery as some sort of recompense? Whatever his motive, we are left with the knowledge that soap has improved the hygiene of the world and provided one of the great commercial enterprises, whose sponsorship and advertising gave its name to radio and TV serials of popular appeal, soap operas.

Art, of course, can last forever. Perhaps Lever's genius lay his advertising campaigns, some of which linked fine paintings to his products. Thus scented soap of many colours entered our culture as more than a mere substance used for washing our bodies.

During his life, Lever had acquired at least 20,000 works of art, many hung or stood in his many houses. Around 12,000 items, ranging from ceramics to furniture, paintings to Roman statues, would form the basis of the Lady Lever collection. The gallery is visited by thousands of local people and tourists every year. A charabanc parked outside is a regular sight.

There are 900 Grade II Listed buildings in the village, Among the finest are the Gladstone Hall/theatre (1891), the Post Office (1894), the Heritage Centre (1896), the Bridge Inn (1900), Christ Church (1902. It can seat 2,000 people) and Hesketh Hall (the Royal British Legion, 1902).

Lever did little dancing down the frivolous walks of life, but his ambition was breathtaking. In 1917, he had bought land in the Western Isles of Lewis and Harris in a bid to improve the local economy. His efforts were not entirely successful, though he had chosen the title of Lord Leverhulme of the Western Isles. He sold this land in 1923.

By then he had embarked on an extraordinary project on his land in Rivington, near his native Bolton, to recreate the ruins of Liverpool Castle. He wanted the building to be seen as it would have been after the damage sustained in the English Civil War. The castle was finished after his death and is now a tourist attraction.

Although he died at his London home, Lord Leverhulme was buried next to his wife at Christ Church, Port Sunlight. He was a man of that time, when successful Britons had a sense of greatness and felt that their ambition should lift others. Think of him sometimes, when you sink into the warmly scented and sighing bubbles of your bath, to ease away the pressures of the day. He was a grand man, but he gave us simple pleasures.

MOLYNEUX FAMILY were of great importance in the early development of Liverpool. Their ancestors came here with the Norman Invasion started by William the Conqueror's victory at Hastings in 1066. The family acquired lands in Lancashire. Their name refers to their home in Molineaux-Sur-Seine, Normandy. They rapidly increased their strength and influence and gained control of Liverpool in the seventeenth century, but their decision to support the Royalist cause in the English Civil War was remembered by townsfolk, who generally backed Cromwell and saw thousands of their fellows die, as Liverpool and its Castle became a battleground.

In 1672, Caryll Molyneux attemped to build a bridge across the Pool linking the ancient port with common land. But this was pulled down by local people led by Edward Marsh and James Whitfield. Their defiant act gave the people of the emerging township control over the port, its land and its businesses. But the Molyneux remained powerful as Lords of the Manor at Sefton. The seat of the Earls of Sefton became Croxteth Hall, which was bequeathed to Liverpool by the 7th and last Earl of Sefton, Hugh William Osbert Molyneux.

EDWARD MARSH and JAMES WHITFIELD. Early examples

of what became the "Scouse" spirit. In 1669, the Molyneux family built a bridge across the original Pool of Liverpool, linking common land to the developed part of the township. Marsh and Whitfield led locals in pulling it down, believing the land should belong to the people. Although they were briefly jailed, the two men gained the support of their fellow citizens and established common rights over the land.

BILLY BUTLER (1942–). Since the introduction of local radio in 1967,

Liverpool has been blessed with outstanding broadcasters.

There is Johnny Kennedy, a man who of many talents – a fine singer, actor and lover of Shakespeare, who can hop from accent to accent as deftly as a frog on a lily pond; Linda McDermott, a brilliant interviewer, writer, lover of literature and dedicated Liverpool patriot; Pete Price, wit and polemicist; Roger Phillips, the master of phone-in shows and a gravel-voiced interviewer of erudition and immense patience; and Spencer Leigh, the magnificent popular music authority, who fills me with fear every time I write on his subject, lest I should make a mistake.

But above them all is Billy, the king of local Radio. He has worked for both the main Liverpool stations – Radio Merseyside, where he is now, and Radio City.

But Billy made his name first on TV, on *Thank Your Lucky Stars*, an ITV show, which had been introduced to compete against the BBC's cleverly named *Juke Box Jury*.

In the early 1960s, people across the generations were interested in whether a new record would be a hit or miss. Hits entered the charts. Misses didn't. *Thank Your Lucky Stars* had a section called Spin-a-Disc, in which young people would be asked their opinion on new releases.

The most famous of the panelists was Janice Nicholls, celebrated for saying "Oi'l give it foive (marks)" in a Midlands accent. For two years Billy was the Scouser on this panel.

Although he had been the singer with several popular groups, Billy was to establish his reputation as the DJ at various Liverpool clubs, most famously the Cavern (from 1964 to 1969). He joined Radio Merseyside in 1971. Listeners knew he was a real Scouser straightaway. In those days regional accents were not as widely accepted, though the success of The Beatles had begun the change that. Yet, it was still quite usual for someone with a posher voice to speak in a regional accent to emphasise a point or to tell a joke.

Billy had an instinctive feel for a radio audience, which is enhanced by his expansive knowledge of popular culture. He has a massive collection of comics from the various generations and can talk about the sweets, biscuits, sherbets, films and their stars, and everyday products popular in the 1950s – at the drop of a pear.

ARTHUR ASKEY (1900–1982) was the most famous of his generation of Liverpool comedians.

Young ears might scoff at the notion of the *Busy, Busy Bee* song, written in 1938 by Kenneth Blain, but little Arthur made it his own, dressing appropriately in wings, as he savoured the witty lines about the glorious bee whiling away the passing hours, pinching all the pollen from the cauliflowers, as well as being "quite a little tease, raising lumps upon the maidens' knees".

Arthur was born in Moses Street, in an area of Liverpool known as the Holy Land because of the biblical street names. He was a bright boy, the son of a book-keeper, and won a scholarship to Liverpool Institute, carving his name on a desk, which would later be filled by Paul McCartney.

Arthur was a keen member of the congregation at St Michael's-in-the-Hamlet parish church, attending Bible classes and singing in the choir, while also taking part in entertainments at school. He became a clerk in the council offices, advising parents on when their children should have their tonsils and adenoids removed – a suitably respectable occupation for someone from his promising background.

Although he was called up for military service in the Great War, it finished before he had experienced serious action. Arthur didn't really like his job as a clerk and he began learning jokes and performing in local concert parties, including his own, the Filberts, before he was recruited into the touring Song Salad Concert Party.

By the late 1930s, he was a minor star, already experienced in pantomime and summer shows. The breakthrough came in 1938, when he was invited to join Richard Murdoch in the BBC series, *Bandwaggon*, which ran for 11 episodes.

The pair supposedly had a flat in the BBC building and from there they launched upon the public the characters of Mrs Bagwash, her daughter Nausea; the pigeons, Basil, Lucy, Ronald and Sarah, as well as Lewis the goat.

In the 1940s, Askey starred in a number of films including *Charley's (Big-Hearted) Aunt, The Ghost Train, I Thank You, King Arthur Was a Gentleman* and *Bees in Paradise*. It was another comic age, in which the stars emerging from music hall still used instantly recognisable catchprases.

Among Askey's was his tag, "I Thank You". TV became another successful outlet for him with his show *Before Your Very Eyes* starting in 1953. For most of the rest of his career, he would appear on stage and TV.

In 1981, he was appointed CBE, a small man with thick-lensed glasses, but a giant on stage. As an old man, who had both legs amputated, he again demonstrated the huge courage that he had needed as a young fellow facing the audiences with only his talent for protection.

TED RAY (1905–1977) was a Liverpool comedian, who had his greatest success on wireless, though he was often seen carrying a violin, which gave him a rather grand image, though he could use the instrument to excellent comic effect. There was no doubt in the public imagination that a violinist was a cut above those "banjo-strummers". Even so, Ray scraped his instrument between films at the Liverpool picture places, being pelted with oranges at one in Scotland Road, always a salutary experience for the up-and-coming comedian.

Ray had seen much of life before he was famous. He was born Charles Olden, the son of Charles and Margaret Olden. Although his father was a skilled craftsman/artist, as the maker of stained glass, some of which is in Liverpool Cathedral, he longed to be a star and performed a comedy routine in pubs, later becoming a landlord himself.

The father advised young Charles that if he learned the violin, he would never be out of work. The son heeded this advice and took violin lessons from a lady teacher in Lower Breck Road, Anfield.

From Anfield Road School, Charles won a scholarship to Liverpool College, a public school, which served the sons of the city's professional and merchant classes, while taking boarders from futher afield. Despite his scholarship, Charles did not shine academically, though he was a whizz at sports, particularly football, where he could dart and weave down the right wing.

For a while, he was an amateur with Liverpool FC, but nothing great came of that. His other ambition to be a motorbike rider at the TT Races on the Isle of Man also fizzled. But he held down a number of jobs, including working as a steward on the ships. Through this time, he was developing his show business potential.

He sang in orchestras as well as playing in the cinemas. In 1933 he changed his name to the snappy Ted Ray, in memory of an American golf champion.

Ted Ray toured the halls with considerable success before the war. However, his style was best suited to radio and in 1949 he began the 10-year run of *Ray's A Laugh*. For 14 years, he was member of the panel game, *Does the Team Think?*

Inevitably TV called and in the mid-fifties, he had his own *Ted Ray Show*. Ted and his wife, Sybil Stevens, a dancer, had two sons, Robin (1934–1998) and Andrew (1939–2003). Robin's success matched that of his father. He taught drama at RADA before pursuing his own career in showbiz, which led to the BBC panel show *Call My Bluff*, which he began chairing in 1965. Like his dad, Robin was a bit of an intellectual and the following year he joined the radio show *Face the Music*, which exercised his remarkable ability to identify composers and pieces of music from very short extracts played on the piano. Good-looking in an unthreatening way, he was ideal for TV quiz shows such as the *Movie Quiz* and *Film Buff of the Year*.

In the late 1960s, he also presented the children's educational TV show, *Sounds Exciting*.

Robin's status in celebrity circles had been enhanced by his marriage to Susan Stranks in 1960. Although an actress, she was best known for presenting the children's TV series *Magpie* between 1968 and 1974. In a modest way, they were a golden couple.

In 1986, Ray's musical, *Café Puccino*, opened at the Wyndham's Theatre, London. In the early 1990s, Ray helped start the radio station, Classic FM, helping choose its playlist.

Andrew Ray was also successful, beginning as the street urchin in the film *Mudlark* (1950) with Alec Guinness and Irene Dunne. He then became a regular on the big screen with leading roloes in such films as *The Yellow Balloon*, *Serious Charge* (with Cliff Richard|) and *Twice Round the Daffodils* (Juliet Mills and Kenneth Williams).

There were difficult times in his career, but he continued on stage winning decent parts on stage and screen, including many TV shows. He was such a superb George VI in *Crown Matrimonial* that he was cast as the stammering younger George (then Duke of York) in the TV series, *Edward and Mrs Simpson* (1978).

ROBB WILTON (1881–1957) was a comedian of the highest order with a slow, dry delivery in the deep tones of an undertaker, which enhanced his immense powers as a storyteller, of the sort you might hear at a bus-stop or bar.

There has always been sympathy for the development of jokes in Liverpool, rather than the slick, fast-shooting gags favoured in London and American cities. In this spirit, it is said that Wilton first used the expression, "To Live in Liverpool you have to be a comedian".

There was in him a mordant understanding of life. In one sketch he was a firemen. "Keep it going until we get there," he said to a caller. His own upbringing in Brownlow Hill was reasonably steady. His father was a newspaper compositor. From school, he played at various local venues, packed with customers prepared to give the acts (or turns) a bad time. You had to be tough to survive. Wilton was tough, but he was also sensitive and highly tuned to the nuances of life.

His career was advanced by the impresario Sir Walter de Frece, who had seen him at the Pavilion theatre, New Brighton. He was soon appearing at all the top venues in this country, as well as touring Australia, Canada and the USA. There were also film parts, as his star continued to rise.

He was at his best when entering the character of British workers, such as the fireman or Home Guardsman, demonstrating an instinctive understanding of the bleak British humour, which runs through the routines of life. Wilton was still much in demand in the early 1950s, just before the old music hall acts were swept aside by rock and roll and then TV. Robb Wilton was often mentioned as an inspiration by the later generations of comedians.

DERYCK GUYLER (1914–1999) was the first person to broadcast the Scouse accent to a mass audience, though the accent he used for Frisby Dyke, a character in the radio show *It's That Man Again* (ITMA), which had been started by his fellow Liverpudlian Tommy Handley (1892–1949) in 1939.

Guyler didn't join the show until 1946. The strange name of his character came from a shop in London Road, Liverpool, which had closed 11 years earlier.

It was perhaps surprising that Guyler should have been associated with a thick Liverpool accent, as he was from a well-to-do background. His father was a jeweller and his mother came from a solid line of professionals.

Deryck was born in Wallasey, but the family crossed the water and he was educated at Liverpool College, the school favoured by the professional and merchant classes. But his accent was nowhere near as "thick" as those heard on more recent TV and radio shows. In his day, actors, who normally had cut-glass voices, put on an accent for particular parts – hence the token working-class "Cockney sparrer" in the old British films.

Anyway, Guyler left school without showing a great deal of promise. However, he had played the drums and the washboard in a kind of proto-skiffle group formed by some of his school pals. After school Guyler, a deeply religious young man, considered a life in the church and converted from Anglicanism to Catholicism, but decided on a secular career working for his father. He then joined Liverpool Repertory in 1935.

During the war he served with ENSA concert parties, where his skill as a washboard-strummer finally paid off. He was taken on by the RAF as a policeman but was invalided out in 1942 because of his defective eyes. He joined the BBC as a newsreader and general broadcaster and this eventually led to ITMA.

Although never a star, Guyler was a steady character actor in numerous radio and TV sit-coms and is particularly remembered for his portrayal of the long-suffering policeman Wilfred "Corky" Turnbull in the popular Sykes TV series, starring Eric Sykes and Hattie Jacques during the 1960s and '70s, as well as Mr Potter, the caretaker in the school series, *Please Sir*, starring John Alderton, from the same period. He was cast as a police inspector in The Beatles' film *A Hard Day's Night* (1964) and as an art professor in *Ferry Cross the Mersey* (1965) with Gerry Marsden and Cilla Black.

BOBBY WILLIS (1942–1999) was a talented singer, musician and songwriter on the Liverpool scene, who married his long-time sweetheart, Cilla Black. He was also her manager and guide. His own song, *Shy of Love*, appeared on the flip side of her first hit, *Love of the Loved* (1963). Another of his songs, *Is It Love?*, was featured in the film, *Ferry Cross the Mersey* (1965), which starred Cilla and Gerry Marsden. Bobby was a first-class manager, who helped Cilla become one of the Britain's most popular family entertainers. His death from cancer was a terrible blow to her. They had three children – Robert, who took over as her manager, Ben and Jack.

JIMMY TARBUCK (1940–). This son of a bookmaker was something of a chancer as a young man, having sharpened his wit at Liverpool schools, which included the eminent St Francis Xaviers.

Without collecting much in the way of certificates, except those for poor attendance, Jimmy's ambitions was to be a footballer or a rock and roller. He tried several garage jobs without sticking at anything. Showbiz called.

Although his star rose with Merseybeat, gap-toothed "Tarby" had been around for several years before that. In 1958, he had been invited to take part in a talent contest at Butlin's holiday camp in Pwllheli, North Wales, after he had heckled other acts. He won several heats, making his way to the national finals in London. He didn't win, but he was on his way.

Tarbuck's early talent was raw and he was inclined to engage hecklers in acrimonious banter, but the promise was immense. Liverpool had a reputation as a funny city and with The Beatles putting it under the national spotlight, it needed a cheeky young comedian. Tarby was ideal.

He knew the groups. He had a Beatles' hairstyle ("hey, tattyhead" was one of his favourite calls) and he was hard and brash, a perfect combination for the time.

In the early days, he had it tough, serving his apprenticeship in clubs and small seaside venues, but the ambition was always there. Fortunes rose dramatically when he was included in the 1963 TV show, *Comedy Bandbox*. He followed that with a successful appearance at the London Palladium, where he would later replace Bruce Forsyth as the compère of *Sunday Night at the London Palladium*. By then Tarby was a huge star. His TV appearances gradually moved from straight stand-up comedy to game shows such as *Winner Takes All*, *Tarby's Frame Game* and *Full Swing*.

Perhaps because of his own early struggles, he has always been a keen charity worker and in 1994 Tarby was appointed OBE. As we entered the new century, he was still very much in demand as a performer and a highly-paid after-dinner speaker, telling stories about golf and the great celebrities of the fairways.

Tarby has had the good sense to stick at what he's good at. Even in the late 1960s, he never followed his contemporaries, such as John Lennon or George Harrison, down the paths of psychedelia.

WILLIAM MASTERS (1887–1983) was internationally renowned as a jazz musician and composer, having started as a music hall enterainer, where he first used his stage name of **GORDON STRETTON**.

He was born to a black father and Irish mother in the Scotland Road area of Liverpool. At the peak of his fame in Europe, he could attract admiring crowds to the leading venues of Paris and London. However, he achieved even greater celebrity in Argentina, as one of the finest exponents of tango music. Some feel, understandably, that he has not received sufficient recognition in his native Liverpool, perhaps because of his colour. This is a justifiable complaint often made by Liverpool's black performers. However, efforts have been made in the twenty-first century to ensure that Gordon Stretton has an honoured place among the great entertainers of the city.

© JEFF DANIELS

CATHERINE "KITTY" WILKINSON (1785–1860) is the saint of Liverpool folk history for her understanding that cleanliness would help check the spread of disease. This resulted in the opening of Britain's first public wash-house in Upper Frederick Street, Liverpool, in 1842.

SILAS HOCKING (1850–1935) was born in Cornwall and became a campaigning clergyman and an influential social commentator, whose great novel, *Her Benny*, about Liverpool urchins, sold more than a million copies in his own lifetime.

JAMES WILLIAM CARLING (1857–1887) was a barefoot pavement artist as a boy, who found a measure of fame and fortune in the USA, before returning to Liverpool, where he died in abject poverty and was buried in a pauper's grave.

HENRY CARLING (1856–1932) was an older brother of James William Carling. He, too, started as a barefooted pavement chalker, but moved to the USA, where he stayed, eventually being recognised as a fine portraitist. In some ways he might have been more talented than his brother, but his story lacks the tragedy, which has given James William Carling a revered place in our folk history.

MICHAEL KELLY (1932–) was born in comparative poverty in the Scotland Road area of Liverpool, where he found that love and decent moral values can help compensate for a lack of material possessions. He was a fine amateur sportsman, who earned his living as a ships' carpenter, before discovering his gift for writing and storytelling. His biography of Kitty Wilkinson, the Liverpool wash-house pioneer, was a local bestseller and he followed that with The Irish Connection, about prominent Liverpudlians of Irish ancestry, and Mothers of the City, which tells of Liverpool women dedicated to the betterment of society. Michael developed into a fine public speaker and became a proprietor of the Liverpool Athenaeum, which was established in 1797 as a place of learning.

© ANTHONY AND LORRAINE BROWN EMSO ARTS

JAMES NUGENT (1822–1905). In the great Victorian tradition of good works, this fine Liverpool priest realised that a lack of education and an insatiable thirst for the temporary consolations of the demon drink combined to block any hope the poor had of advancing.

His own family circumstances were comparatively easy despite his parents, John and Mary, having nine children, of whom he was the eldest. They ensured that he received a decent educational grounding and he trained for the priesthood at the English College in Rome, before being ordained into St Nicholas' church, Liverpool, in 1846.

His great concern was the future of the thousands of poor children begging on the streets of what was growing into a mighty port. To this end he opened the ragged School on Copperas Hill, where the children were offered food, shelter and clothing, as well as books. This was followed by his Industrial School, which taught various trades and continued until 1923. He was also influential in the development of the Catholic Institute on Hope Street, which later became St Edward's College, one of Liverpool's top schools.

Realising that the fate of some children was beyond hope in Liverpool, he pioneered Canadian emigration in the 1860s and 1870s, finding homes for thousands of children in the New World. He also helped to found a refuge in the Dingle, serving women who had been released from prison. His work is continued by the Nugent Care Society.

Frederick William Pomeroy's statue of Father Nugent, who became a monsignor in 1890, was paid for by public subscription and unveiled in 1906, in St John's Gardens at the back of St George's Hall, where it still stands. The Inscription on the base says, "Save the Boy".

Inscribed on the left side of the plinth are his own words: "Speak a kind word, take them gently by the hand, work is the best reforming and elevating power, loyalty to the country and God."

On the rear, it says: "An eye to the blind, a foot to the lame, the father of the poor."

On the right it has the following tribute to Nugent: "The apostle of temperance, the protector of the orphan child, the consoler of the prisoner, the reformer of the criminal, the saviour of fallen womanhood, the friend of all in poverty and affliction."

CARL BERNARD BARTELS (1866–1955) was a German-born woodcarver living in England, who won a competition for the design of the Liver Birds on top of the Royal Liver Building, which opened in 1911. He has received little official recognition in the city. His German ancestry meant that he was detained as a prisoner in the Knockaloe camp on the Isle of Man during the Great War. At the time anti-German sentiments were running high in Liverpool, which could explain the lack of recognition for Bartels.

GLENDA JACKSON (1936–). I met Glenda on a miserable Sunday afternoon in 1983 when she was officially opening a theatre that had been named after her on the campus of the old Birkenhead Technical College, a concrete and brick, multi-storey oblong about a mile and a half from her birthplace in Market Street, off the town centre.

I had been commissioned to cover the event by the Manchester office of the *Daily Telegraph* and was joined by Tony Storey, an old pal from the *Birkenhead News*. After a spirited performance of *Jesus Christ Superstar*, the musical by Andrew Lloyd Webber and Tim Rice, we joined Glenda and some civic dignitaries for drinks and canapes. Several of the local bigwigs struggled with the word canapes and pronouced it as "can apes", as in "can apes speak better than politicians?", but Birkenhead wasn't so sophisticated in those days with most locals still preferring Rhyl to the Cote d'Azur, quite rightly in my opinion.

Glenda, who had been made a Commander of the British Empire in 1978, did her stuff, shaking hands and making small talk with strangers about her films, some of which had included remarkably bold sex scenes for the period. But, for her, this had been another performance of the polite local girl made good and being eternally grateful to the town of her birth. After a while, however, she gestured to me and Tony, indicating with hand movements that she would like to go outside for a fag and a chinwag. Although she was reasonably diplomatic, it was obvious from her tone that she felt ill at ease at VIP parties, not because she had been included on the guest list, but because of those who had been excluded – often the men and women whose labour had made the event possible. That had been true at the the great launching ceremonies held about half a mile away at the Cammell Laird shipyard. You rarely saw more than a token worker at the celebratory feasts. She was, of course, in simple form expressing her passion for social justice, which was most likely to be achieved through socialism, or so she would have argued then (and still would, I suppose).

I was a youngish man at the time and felt that it was quite an honour to be smoking outside a college in Birkenhead with one of the most successful actresses in the country – indeed, one who had been prepared to unrobe for her art. She was very slim with a rather severe manner, which was broken every now and again by a big smile, offered in appreciation of a joke or black observation. Given her slim stature, her voice was unexpectedly strong and husky and it carried a hint of the school mistress in a tone, hardly touched by the vowels of Merseyside.

Sadly, the theatre and the college were demolished about 20 years later to make room for houses.

The circumstances of her childhood would have sharpened Glenda's awareness of social divides. She was the first daughter of the bricklayer Harry Jackson and his wife Joan. From Market Street, the family had moved about seven miles to Hoylake, generally a more genteel setting, where she was brought up with her sisters, Gill, Lynn and Elizabeth. It was a lively household in a little town that had remained a small residential holiday resort with a much larger day-trip trade – a modestly refined answer to the popularity of New Brighton. Glenda attended West Kirby Grammar School for girls, which attracted bright pupils from across the social spectrum. She was not particularly academic, but she had begun acting and dancing at the local YMCA and this eventually led to her entering RADA in 1955, after spells working as a shop assistant with Boots the chemist and Woolworth's.

She trained at RADA for four years, but certainly didn't find instant stardom, working in repertory in Worthing and Crewe and gaining small parts on TV and in the film, *This Sporting Life* (1963) – as a singer at a party. She was then with the Royal Shakespeare Company for four years, working under the director, Peter Brook. In this time, her interest in politics remained strong. Fame came suddenly with Ken Russell's interpretation of the DH Lawrence novel, *Women in Love* (1969). Even for the "swinging sixties" it was extraordinarily sexually explicit, making the point, almost never heard in popular entertainment, that women had carnal desires. Glenda's portrayal of Gudrun Brangwen won her an Academy Award as best actress. The following year she made *Sunday, Bloody Sunday*, which was another critical success. Also in 1970, she appeared as Tchaikovsky's desperately frustrated wife in another Russell film, the *Music Lovers*, which, to coin the modern phrase, "contained nudity", most notably in a railway scene, in which she tried to seduce her reluctant groom (Richard Chamberlain). To Britain's vast armchair audience, the peak of her career was achieved with a meticulously controlled portrayal of Elizabeth in the BBC's acclaimed series, *Elizabeth R* (1971). But she would win another academy award in 1974 for the comedy, *A Touch of Class*. Her career continued to flourish with such films as *The Triple Echo* and her wonderfully sympathetic interpretation of the poet, Stevie Smith, in *Stevie* (1978).

But film did not satisfy her political needs, even if it had given her a prominent place on the liberal and artistic left of British society.

In 1992, she was elected the Labour member for Hampstead and Highgate, a constituency long associated with the more soft-palmed, intellectual wing of the party. Seven years later she was appointed junior minister for London Transport in Tony's Blair's first government, but in 2000 she was unsuccessful in her bid to be the Labour candidate for the election to pick the first Mayor of London. Glenda's passion remains politics. She is usually to the left of her party and was vehemently opposed to the war against Iraq. Despite all the glory and the gongs, Glenda is working-class girl from Birkenhead. She has done well, but she wants to live in a country of opportunity for children from all backgrounds.

KAY KELLY (1944–2010), the daughter of Frank and Kay Peeney, was brought up on Sumner Street, the fifth of their six children. Her mother later remarried and had another five children. After an education at St Sylvester's School and St Mary's School, Highfield Street, she had factory and shop jobs. She was only 18 when she married Pat Kelly, a docker, who later worked on bus maintenance. They had four children. Pat died in 2005, having been nursed though cancer by Kay at their home in Everton. Kay embodied the old community spirit and has been one of the most effective campaigners in Liverpool's recent history.

"Some people think I'm a pain in the bum," she admitted, proudly. For petty officials were her enemy. She brought help to hundreds of people, who had been the victims of bureaucratic indifference. Fuelled by a profound faith in the teachings of Christ, she was less enthusiastic about some of his represent-atives on Earth. Kay was old Liverpool through and through. She didn't feel that much of the prosperity found in the "new" city, which was the European Capital of Culture in 2008, had benefited ordinary people. She died in March 2010 from a complication arising from her lung condition, which had held off for more than 30 years, allowing her to continue with her community work. A funeral mass was held for her at the Metropolitan Cathedral of Christ the King (Liverpool's Catholic Cathedral). Among those offerering praise for her work on Earth was the Most Reverend Patrick Kelly, Archbishop of Liverpool. Many prayed that she was now in the care of her devoted friend, the Virgin Mary.

BERYL MARSDEN (1947–). Whatever happened to …? Unfortunately, she does find herself in those listings from time to time. But she shouldn't. Most of the old Merseybeat stars and their followers freely admit that Beryl was the best female singer around in those days and she still is around – performing and recording.

The press said that her great rival was Cilla Black, who had enjoyed far more commercial success, having quite quickly established herself as an all-round entertainer in the old style.

But neither woman has ever engaged in this debate and they didn't know each other in the Cavern days. However, it was reasonable to note that they were both Liverpool girls, trying to break through in an industry dominated by men.

In late 1966, it seemed that Beryl did have a chance, not only to match Cilla commercially, but to be recognised as the more "hip" artist. She was the female singer in a group called Shotgun Express. The other members were Rod Stewart (vocals), Peter Bardens (organ), Peter Green (guitar), Phil Sawyer (guitar), Dave Ambrose (bass) and Mick Fleetwood (drums). Well, Rod went on to be one of the greatest rocks stars to emerge from these shores, while Green and Fleetwood formed Fleetwood Mac and Bardens joined Love Affair and then formed Village. These men were then musicians on the brink.

As Shotgun Express, they released a single called, *I Could Feel the World Turn Round*, which, though a little over-produced, wasn't a bad vehicle for her singing alongside Rod. Its failure to make the national charts, despite being popular with some DJs, probably hurried the group's break-up after some stormy months in 1967.

Beryl, still very much in touch with trends, then joined an all female group called She Trinity, featuring Robyn Yorke (drums), Janet Bailey (also drums), Pauline Moran (bass), Eileen Woodman (keyboards) and Barbara Thompson (sax). But again there was no great commercial success.

Beryl Hogg, as she was born in Carter Street, Toxteth, had nine siblings. From an early age, she sang and her professional career began when she was only 15. The Undertakers, one of the most popular and accomplished groups on Merseyside, were playing at a local venue. At the instigation of friends, she joined them on stage and, from this impromptu performance, became their regular singer, though she was too young to join them at the Star Club, Hamburg, where The Beatles had made such a lasting impression. She had adopted the name Marsden after Bill Marsden, who managed a venue in Birkenhead. She was not related to Gerry Marsden, as was supposed by some people.

Brian Epstein expressed an interest in managing her. Instead, she was taken on by Joe Flannery, his showbiz partner, and her local career continued to flourish. She sang with Lee Curtis and the All Stars. The late Bob Wooler, legendary DJ at the Cavern, said after the glory years, "I preferred her to Cilla. If Brian (Epstein) had taken Beryl she would have been a big-seller."

Then, when she was 17, Beryl moved to the management of Tony Stratton-Smith, a sports writer, who had entered the music scene.

Beryl's real problem had been finding the right song. None of her singles were hits and, at that time, hits were crucial to the success of pop singers. A small figure at just five feet and one inch, she was full of verve with a great vocal style and bags of sex appeal – as was noted by a string of lovers, including Keith Richards of The Rolling Stones. Her personal life has often been tempestuous or "colourful", as the newspapers would say; but her Buddhist faith, coupled with a great deal of experience, has settled her life in more recent times. Through it all, Beryl has retained the affection and respect of her contemporaries to a remarkable extent.

ROSE HEILBRON (1914–2005).

"I want no *judy* defending me," said the hard man accused of a murder that had chilled the blood of decent society. He almost spat out the slang word used instead of girl or woman and then in vogue in Liverpool. But this was a woman who met prejudice in rather the same way as a hobnailed boot meets a beetle, though she possessed a great deal more finesse – and a generous share of good looks. But a brilliant brain was the instrument of her success. "Nothing gets past her," was another local expression that encapsulated the remarkable mental agility that would turn young Miss Heilbron into one of the greatest lawyers of her generation.

Rose was the second daughter of Max Heilbron, a Jewish hotelier, who had run a boarding house for refugees. His wife, Nellie, died in 1938, causing Rose and her elder sister, Anne, much grief. By then, however, the course of

Rose's life was set. She had been educated at Liverpool's Belvedere School, which had been established as the Liverpool High School in 1880, the year Liverpool became a city. The school was for the daughters of Liverpool's strongly emerging middle-class. In the tone of this school, one might have detected shades of the Marcia Blaine School of Edinburgh, created by Muriel Spark for her novel, *The Prime of Miss Jean Brodie*.

Rose studied law at Liverpool University, graduating with first-class honours in 1935, leading the way to her Master's degree in law and a series of firsts – the first women to win a Scholarship to Gray's Inn, the first women to be appointed a King's Counsel, first women to lead in a murder case, first women judge to sit at the Old Bailey and the first women treasurer of Gray's Inn (one of the four Inns of Court in London, professional associations for judges and barristers). In 1974, she was appointed a Dame of the British Empire.

Despite all these triumphs, Rose Heilbron's name is remembered most in Liverpool for her defence of George Kelly. On March 19, 1949, Leonard Thomas, 44, and Bernard Catterall, 30, the manager and assistant manager of the Cameo cinema in Wavertree, Liverpool, had been shot dead while refusing to release the night's takings of more than £50 to a masked gunman.

With national outrage mounting against armed crime, much fanned by the popular Press, the investigating police officers were under great pressure to bring the culprit/culprits to justice. They scoured the underbelly of the city, interviewing pimps, prostitutes, stool-pigeons and criminals, in their bid to build up a case.

In fact, on the basis of some dubious evidence from these underworld sources, they were able to charge George Kelly, 27, with shooting the men and Charles Connolly, 26, with organising the raid and acting as the lookout. They were tried at Liverpool Assizes in St George's Hall. The trial ran for 13 days. Although Kelly and Connolly were not men to excite much sympathy, the prosecution case against them was not convincing. Both men had alibis for that night. The jury could not reach verdicts and a retrial was ordered. In the interim, further evidence of an even more doubtful nature had been unearthed.

Rose took on the defence of Kelly, a minor criminal with a formidable appearance, who had on occasions been dubbed "Little Caesar".

"I want no judy defending me," he told her. But she persisted. In the end her brilliant submissions failed and he was hanged by Albert Pierrepoint and his assistant, Harry Allen, at Walton Prison, Liverpool, on March 28, 1950. But, in part because of her stirling performance in the Cameo case, Rose was named the *Daily Mirror*'s Woman of the Year.

At the second trial, Connolly, pleaded guilty to robbery and conspiracy and was sentenced to 10 years in gaol.

Rose Heilbron's inner sense about Kelly's innocence was proved correct in 2003 when the Court of Appeal quashed the convictions of both men as unsafe.

People argued that her remarkable rise had been aided by the large number of male lawyers leaving their offices to serve in the Second World War. It was also argued that her medical expertise, used with notable effect in many cases, had been assisted by her marriage in 1945 to Nathaniel Burstein, a Dublin-born doctor, with whom she would have a daughter, Hilary, also a QC. There was truth in these points, but clever people take advantage of the few opportunities offered in life.

The achievements of Rose Heilbron are best appreciated when measured against the barriers then placed before ambitious women.

LIZZIE CHRISTIAN (1898–1977). Her face was brighter than the wild flowers of those free hills, seen in picture postcards – far away from her own home in Liverpool. And in the defiance of that face, rising unflinchingly above her stalls of vegetables and fruit and dazzling daffodils, there was the spirit of people, who did not bow easily to others.

For Lizzie was our barrow girl – the first of 12 children born to docker James Hawker and his wife Rebecca Paroni, who lived in a small terraced house near Brownlow Hill, site of the old workhouse. From the start, her life was harsh, but she was tough – a lot tougher than the soft leather shoes worn by the toffs, who took bouquets home to their wives or sweethearts.

She had married "handsome" Jack Christian, a soldier who left her with seven children, all of whom she loved and they loved her. In all this time of toil and worry, she never drank or smoked or saw "a moving picture show". The barrow was her world – small, usually wearing a headscarf and an old mac, she had a pitch near Liverpool's Central station. From time to time, she would be moved because of new developments or at the whim of bureaucrats. During her years she also had pitches in St John's precinct, Casey Street and Clayton Square. As ill-health, doubtless worsened by days at her barrow in the freezing fog, took its toll, Lizzie edged towards retirement – often reminding people of the time a "cowboy" had paid for her taxi home. The cowboy was PJ Proby, a great singing star, who had been appearing at the Wooky Hollow night club.

Yes, you can talk of the Mona Lisa with her enigmatic smile and you can stroll the portrait galleries of the world. But you will never see a face like that of our Lizzie Christian, staring at you from another age. She is forever Liverpool.

AGNES JONES (1832–1868). The undertaker's tape became a worn and frayed tool in the fetid hovels of Victorian Liverpool, where the smell of death was as familiar to the nostrils as gin on the breath of the shawlies sitting on those doorsteps – so often crossed by priests with their holy thumbs, prayer books and incantations for the next world.

But Agnes Jones was more concerned about the people left destitute and ill in this world. For she played a role in the development of nursing in Britain that in many ways was as important as that of the more celebrated Florence Nightingale (1820-1910), the Lady with the Lamp from the Crimean War. After that war had ended in 1856, Florence had been granted £50,000 to set up an insititution for the training of nurses at St Thomas's Hospital, London. This resulted in her book, Notes of Nursing. In this period, men and women of social conscience were deeply ashamed that Britain should have so much poverty and wretchedness at home, as it embarked on building an empire that would become the biggest and the wealthiest the world had known. Such a man was William Rathbone, the Liverpool merchant, philanthropist and admirer of Florence Nightingale, who would serve as the Liberal MP for Liverpool between 1862 and 1880.

In 1865, he had written to Florence expressing his deep concern about the hospital at the Liverpool workhouse on Brownlow Hill, suggesting that he could help finance a team of nurses to improve conditions there. Could she suggest a suitable woman to lead them? Florence suggested her friend Agnes Jones, who, like her, had been born into comparative privilege.

Agnes was born in Cambridge, the daughter of Lieutenant Colonel Joseph Jones of Kildare and his wife, Elizabeth Smyth of Ardmore, County Derry. They returned to Ireland during Agnes's childhood and set up home in the spacious and lushly-lawned Fahan House, Fahan, County Derry. Despite her lofty position in local society, Agnes seemed driven by a calling to help the needy. They were her people – rather than the giddy young women who preened and simpered beneath the chandeliers at the grand balls. After an education in Dublin and Stratford-upon-Avon, Agnes toured Europe in 1853, visiting the Kaiserwerth Institution in Bonn, where new nursing methods were being practised. Florence had been a student there two years earlier. Three years later, Agnes took up a post at the Dublin Hospital, but spent more time working with the destitute on the streets. These experiences taught her that kindness and rudimentary nursing were not enough. She needed more medical expertise. So, in 1862, she registered as a student Nightingale Nurse at St Thomas's. Her potential was apparent from the start and before long she was appointed superintendent of the Great Northern Hospital, London. While Agnes was working there, Florence received Rathbone's letter. This resulted in the Select Vestry (committee) appointing her superintendent of the workhouse hospital in 1864. She took up the post the following year, by which time Rathbone and his friends had decorated and furnished a room for her.

The passage of time makes it difficult to even imagine what conditions were like in the poor quarters of Victorian Liverpool. Many suffered with stoical forebearance, hoping for better things in the next world. But the stench of horse and human waste and rotting food would have hung like a pall over the grossly overcrowded, unsanitised courtyards. Death was part of life, evident for all to see. But we shouldn't think only of what the philanthopists called the "deserving poor". Violent drunks, rapists, child-molesters, robbers, footpads, prostitutes, soap-box politicians, crazed preachers, beggars, pimps and dice-rollers paraded the streets, or skulked in the shadowed alleys. Liverpool was a dangerous port and for many people life was cheap You did what you could because time was short. By contrast, Agnes cherished life. In this, she was generously supported by the Rathbones and other upper-middle class families of similar outlook. They were determined that goodness and decency should prevail in Liverpool. In 1880 one of their dreams came true when Liverpool was made a city – sometimes dubbed the second city of the British Empire. But if the other noble ambitions of the well-heeled "Liverpolitans" were to be realised, there had to be a major improvement in the housing, health and education of the common people.

To an extent, we can see Agnes as a pioneering hospital matron – the forerunner of those ladies in starched uniforms who swished down the wards, checking the watches pinned above their breasts, while insisting that the junior nurses should apply a near military precision to their duties, cleanliness running godliness a very close second, if not actually winning. And she was right. Wretched conditions in the hospital and workhouse had played a baleful part in allowing typhus, cholera and other diseases to spread. A team of 12 nurses, who would soon be supported by 65 "able-bodied" assistants, began destroying the filthy bedding and rags, replacing them with clean sheets and blankets. The dead and dying were kept apart from those who still had a chance of recovery. Wounds and sores were cleaned and dressed and, where possible, more space was put between the beds to lessen the risk of infections being passed on. In fact, she had introduced the ideas of hygienic and loving care, which are still at the heart of good nursing.

Of course, it wasn't enough to save everyone and Agnes herself caught typhus in early 1868. Staff, patients and inmates of the workhouse lined the stairways, as her body was carried from the grim building. A cross of white camellias was fastened to the coffin of this most God-fearing woman. She was taken by boat and road to a grave in Fahan, where the young men laid wild flowers over her. Rathbone commissioned a 10ft marble statue of her called the Angel of the Resurrection, sculpted by the Italian Pietro Tenerani. It is now kept in the oratory at Liverpool's Anglican Cathedral. A stained glass window is dedicated to her memory at the cathedral.

ETHEL AUSTIN (1900–1989). She was a business empress from a terraced street, who had never studied the catwalks of Rome or Paris, but her ambition and sound business savvy helped her bring fashions to the ordinery people, her people.

She was born Ethel Laycock, at the turn of a century that would bring hunger, weapons of mass destruction, two world wars, motor cars, family telephones, Communist revolutions, the downfall of great royal families, the rise of political thugs, radio, television, and, in its second half, unimaginable prosperity and the easy life – though these benefits didn't reach everyone, even in the affluent West.

Her childhood home was in Cockburn Street, Dingle, a traditional, working-class area of the city. Ethel was the fifth of nine children. Her parents, Edwin and Mary, were poor, but religiously respectable, and his earnings at various times as a butcher, a cooper and as a docker, ensured that they were never destitute. Even so, it seems that young Ethel was determined to strive for better things. From school, she worked as a shop assistant and then in a paper factory. But her eyes were constantly on the future and that came into view one day when she was boating on Sefton Park lake and met George Auston, a dashing fellow, who had lied about his age so that he could enlist with the Liverpool pals and serve in Flanders during the Great War, which he had survived to become a tram driver. Her parents seemed opposed to an early marriage. However, after years in the trenches serving his country, George had obeyed enough orders. The couple were married at Toxteth Park registrar's office in May 1920. Their son, Ronald, was born the next year, followed by daughters, Lesley and Glenys, Lesely died from septicaemia in 1936 and their last child, Graeme, was born two years later.

By then the family fortunes had suddenly improved. In 1934 an insurance policy of George's had matured giving them what was then a considerable sum of £50. After discussion, her early ambition to use the money for a flower shop was rejected in favour of a wool shop, which would benefit from her expertise as a knitter.

So they rented small premises on Bishop Road, Anfield, with young Ronald pushing a promotional leaflet about the shop through letter boxes in the neighborhood. They called the shop Ethel Austin. With George's wages still coming in to meet household bills, the family was able to buy wool, knitting needles and patterns for clothes. George looked after the financial side of their little business and the couple began to expand their stock, opening a bigger shop in Walton Village, developing the sort of inexpensive stock that would make her a household name on Britain's high streets – underwear, hosiery, clothers for babies and children. Although the war years were difficult with people mending and patching old clothes rather than buying new ones, the business survived and in 1945, Ethel Austin opened another shop on Walton Breck Road and then one on Church Road, Litherland. This was followed by their largest shop so far in Old Swan in 1948. Their little business had become big.

A party was held for staff at a Reece's restaurant that year. It was in Ethel Austin's original spirit – friendship and respect among those to drawn to the original idea of providing her neighbours with sensible, good value clothes.

Although the business continued to expand, Ethel increasingly left the management of the stores to her husband and their son, Ronald. The company celebrated its golden anniversary in 1984 with a party for staff from 65 stores at the Adelphi Hotel. Ethel died five years later. When the shop was sold in 2002, there were more than 200 stores. But it went into administration in 2010, following a serious downturn in sales caused, in part at least, by the international banking crisis that had begun in 2008.

CHARLOTTE (LOTTIE) DOD (1871–1960).

In her day, in polite society, horses sweated, men perspired and women glowed. Well, it might not be impolite to suggest that the occasional pearl of sweat dampened the head of Lottie Dod, the pin up girl of British sport in the late Victorian era. For, in the record books at least, her achievements far outstrip any female athlete of the modern age. Tennis was the sport that turned this girl from the suburbs into a star. If she had been born in modern times, once could easily imagine the rapturous writing that her presence would have stirred from reporters on the *Daily Mail*. Although she never faced the rocket-like serves unleashed by today's players with shoulders like dray horses, Lottie was a keen competitor, who realised that the ball had to be thwacked, rather than patted, if you were to overwhelm your rivals. Before her, tennis had rarely raised itself much above the peaches, cream and strawberries of the courting rituals enjoyed by boys and girls from the privileged classes.

Perhaps, when assessing Lottie, some writers have concentrated too much on her background and not her successes. Her father, Joseph had made a fortune from cotton and banking. With his wife, Margaret, he established an estate called Edgeworth in Bebington. Lottie and her older siblings, Anne, Tony and Willy, had every opportunity to develop their natural talent for sport. Ice-skating, chess, billiards, golf, archery and, of course, tennis were among the games/sports at which they excelled. Tony was an Olympic gold medal winner at archery in 1908. In the same Games, Lottie won a silver medal for archery.

But tennis has a special place in British hearts. "Who's for tennis?" being the mating call of dizzy young people. At the higher level, the Press, then as now, loved personal rivalry and, on the sweet lawns of England, this was provided by Lottie and Blanche Bingley Hillyard (Hillyard being her married name). Blanche (1863-1946) from Ealing was the Wimbledon champion in 1886, 1889, 1894, 1897, 1899 and 1900. But she could not beat our Lottie. They met in the final in 1887, 1888, 1891, 1892 and 1893. Lottie won each time, losing only one set in the 1893 match which ended 6-8, 6-1, 6-4. In the style of the day Lottie served underarm, though her ground strokes and comparative agility on the court were much praised and feared by opponents. Her dresses and blouses were also much admired at the time, but now they would seem to be ludicrously bulky and an obvious impediment in long rallies.

Lottie never married and she spent her last years at a nursing home in Sway, Hampshire, where she died while listening to a Wimbledon commentary on the radio. In 1983 she was inducted into the International Tennis Hall of Fame.

FELICIA HEMANS (1793–1835). If you are remembered for only one line, you might think, 'Well, that's not much return for my life on Earth', but then you might think for a little longer and conclude that most people are not remembered for saying anything. In the light of that consideration, one line, known to almost everyone in the country, becomes something rather special.

The line is of course from Felicia Dorothea Hemans's poem, *Casabianca* – "The boy stood on the burning deck ..."

Now here's a test. What is the next line? Isn't it like one of those songs when everyone joins in the beginning and then has to hum or "la-la" along?

Actually, the next line is: "Whence all but he had fled..."

And it a grand poem full of vivid images, the thunder and glory of war tempered by deep sorrow at the loss of life. Even more remarkably, for the time, the poem is in praise of an enemy. For Casabianca, the boy on the deck, was the son of an officer on the French flagship, *L'Orient*, which came under a merciless attack from Lord Nelson's men during the Battle of the Nile in 1798. He stood at his post, defiantly and passively, during a barrage from 2,000 guns. Finally fire reached the powder magazine on the ship and he was killed in the ensuing explosion.

Although more refined, the poem is in the derring-do spirit of the time, save for the detail about the boy being on an enemy ship. If you had not known it had been written by a women, you might well have supposed it was the work of a man, glorifying bravery. Perhaps, though, the female touch is found in that in sympathy for the boy.

Felicia Hemans was the fifth of seven children born to George Browne, an Irish wine merchant, and his wife, Felicity Wagner, daughter of the consul for Austria and Tuscany in Liverpool. Her childhood home was on the affluent Duke Street, but the family business failed at the turn of the century, in part because of the war against France and they moved to an isolated house in Gwrych North Wales, later moving to St Asaph.

The Hemans were cultured and artistic people with a well-stocked library. Young Felicia spent some time in London, where she met painters and sculptors, though her own gift lay in words. Her first volume of poems was published when she was only 14 and included the epic poem, *England and Spain (Valour and Patriotism)*. Much of her work was in the patriotic, even jingoistic, vein, but her embrace was wide, touching a love of nature, romanticism and popular sentiment. Much of her output was published in magazines and annuals and she was for a while one of the most widely read writers in the English language. In 1811 she married the Irishman Alfred Hemans, an Army captain, and they had five sons before separating.

She is no longer a fashionable poet. Her values belong in another era, but there is an elegance there rarely found in the poets of today. After *Casabianca*, *The Homes of England* is probably her most quoted work.

> The stately Homes of England,
> How beautiful they stand!
> Amid their tall ancestral trees,
> O'er all the pleasant land.
> The deer across their greensward bound
> Thro' shade and sunny gleam,
> And the swan glides past with the sound
> Of some rejoicing stream ...

It's a long way from the ice cream wrappers and the sweating burgers of today's stately homes. Maybe we should be relieved that time shielded her shy sensibilities from the processions of trippers, heading for the "lavvies" and the trinket shops. She she lies in St Ann's Church vaults, Dublin, the city of her later years.

This is an alphabetical list of all those
who appear in this book.

John Peel 113
Roger Peterson 123
Tom Petty 98
Roger Phillips 137
Edgar Allan Poe 55
Frederick William Pomeroy 145
Pope John Paul II 131
Duffy Power 87
John Prescott 95
Billy Preston 99
Elvis Presley 11, 23, 116, 120, 122, 129
Dickie Pride 87

Roy Race of the Rovers 73
William Ratcliffe 83
William Rathbone 152, 153
William Rawson 51
Andrew Ray 140
Robin Ray 140
Ted Ray 118, 139, 140
The Remo Four (Merseybeat group)
    25, 106
Malvina Reynolds 106
Tim Rice 145
Cliff Richard 87, 140
John Brooke Richardson 128
Thomas Rickman 8
Andy Roberts 113
Rikki and the Red Streaks
    (Merseybeat group) 107
Anne Mackenzie Robertson 50
Struan Rodger 128
The Rolling Stones 149
Betty Rowson 7
Earl Royce and the Olympics
Prince Rupert 121
Ken Russell 147
Leon Russell 99

Siegfried Sassoon 105
Phil Sawyer 148
Andrew Schofield 96
Ronnie Scott 106

The Searchers (Merseybeat group)
    25, 105–107, 122
Walter Carruthers Sellar 34, 133
William Shakespeare 53, 90, 137, 147
Ravi Shankar 99
Bill Shankly 26, 75, 122
Helen Shapiro 117
Edward Shaw 104
Sharon Sheeley 122
David Sheppard 33, 131
Wallis Simpson 46
Frank Sinatra 120
Nancy Sinatra 95
Molly Smith 46
Phil Spector 119
Freddie Starr 106, 114
Ringo Starr 16, 88, 124
Thomas Steers 28, 38
Rod Stewart 148
Tony Storey 146
Rory Storm and the Wild Ones 107
Susan Stranks 140
Ronald Neil Stuart 83
Dean Sullivan 96
Stu Sutcliffe 106
Swinging Blue Jeans (Merseybeat
    group) 25
Eric Sykes 142

Jimmy Tarbuck 86, 142
Nel Tarleton 95
Henry Tate 32, 128
Alistair Taylor 115
"Pa" Taylor 94
Alfred, Lord Tennyson 108
Margaret Thatcher 33, 79, 119, 130,
    131
Dylan Thomas 108, 110
Walter Aubrey Thomas 57
Barbara Thompson 149
J.R.R. Tolkien 113
Alex Troupe 2

GREAT
LIVERPUDLIANS

This is a Liverpool history with a difference. Packed with information, this lively book is not only about events but about people – our Great Liverpudlians – and the part they each played in shaping the city.

There are many familiar faces, of course, but they stand shoulder to shoulder with the ordinary men and women who have made Liverpool what it is. And as well as bringing the unsung heroes and their interesting lives to our attention, *Daily Post* columnist David Charters has also dug deep to unearth less well known details about those famous names we all thought we knew everything about.

Great Liverpudlians takes the reader on a wonderfully enjoyable journey through the city's past, introducing us to an array of colourful characters, from kings and politicians, to philanthropists, poets, musicians, comedians, sportsmen and women, barrow girls and clergy.

All human life is here, as they say, and what is any great city if not the sum of its people?

www.palatinebooks.com

£8.95

9 781874 181705

Introduction

Chatham House Publishers, Inc.
Box One, Chatham, NJ 07928

ISBN 1-56643-012-7

900

EAN

9 781566 430128

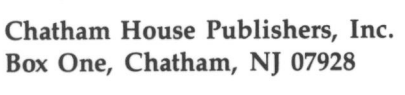